The Son Rises:
The Historical Evidence
for the Resurrection of Jesus

The Son Rises: The Historical Evidence for the Resurrection of Jesus

by
William Lane Craig

Wipf and Stock Publishers
EUGENE, OREGON

All Scripture quotations, except those noted otherwise, are from the *New American Standard Bible,* © 1960, 1962, 1963, 1968, 1971, 1972, 1973, 1975, and 1977 by The Lockman Foundation, and are used by permission.

Scripture quotations indicated "Phillips" are reprinted with permission of Macmillan Publishing Co., Inc. from *The New Testament in Modern English,* Revised Edition by J.B. Phillips, Translator. ©J.B. Phillips 1958, 1960, 1972. These quotations are also used with permission of Collins Publishers, London.

Selected lines are quoted from Archibald MacLeish, "The End of the World," in *New and Collected Poems, 1917-1976,* copyright ©1976 by Archibald MacLeish, and are reprinted by permission of Houghton-Mifflin Company.

Quotations from an essay by Loren Eiseley are reprinted with permission from "The Cosmic Orphan," *Encyclopedia Britannica,* 15th ed. Copyright 1974 by Encyclopedia Britannica, Inc.

The use of selected references from various versions of the Bible in this publication does not necessarily imply publisher endorsement of the versions in their entirety.

Wipf and Stock Publishers
199 West 8th Avenue, Suite 3
Eugene, Oregon 97401

The Son Rises
Historical Evidence for the Resurrection of Jesus
By Craig, William Lane
Copyright©1981 Craig, William Lane
ISBN: 1-57910-464-9
Publication date: September, 2000
Previously published by Moody Press, 1981.

To
Bill and Joan Hartseil
and
all the brothers and sisters

whose love and prayers
were our constant resource
throughout the course of this research

Contents

PREFACE

This is a book for those who may believe in some kind of God or Supreme Being, but doubt whether He has revealed Himself to us in any decisive way.

I am of the firm conviction that God has revealed Himself in a decisive way in history, namely, in the resurrection of Jesus, and that there is solid historical evidence for that fact. This book summarizes that evidence. It is the result of two years of research at the Universität München, West Germany, and at Cambridge University, England, as a fellow of the Alexander von Humboldt Foundation. The Humboldt Foundation, funded by the West German government, is designed to bring scientists and other scholars to Germany to do research at German universities and laboratories. I am extremely grateful to the Humboldt Foundation for the generous grant that funded my research on the historical credibility of the resurrection of Jesus, and I praise God for providing me with this unique opportunity. I also wish to thank my wife, Jan, for her support during the course of the research and for her long hours of work in producing the typescript.

In this book, I attempt to summarize the results of my research in simple, concise terminology, easily understandable to the man on the street. At the same time, however, I have done my best to be thorough and accurate. It is not always easy to do both. A historical investigation of the resurrection of Jesus necessarily involves many very complex issues. The average reader, who has scarcely ever opened the New Testament, much less read it, will no doubt find certain concepts new and difficult to understand. I recommend, therefore, that you read the book slowly and think about it as you go along. I have deliberately avoided specialist terminology and sought to explain everything that might be new to the average reader. Anyone who wishes to pursue these issues more deeply should consult my forthcoming works: *The Historical Argument for the Resurrection of Jesus* and *The Historicity of the Resurrection*.

In considering the historical evidence for the resurrection of Jesus, it is important to avoid giving the impression that the Christian faith is based on the evidence for Jesus' resurrection. The Christian faith is based on the *event* of the resurrection. It is not based on the *evidence* for the resurrection. This distinction is crucial. The Christian faith stands or falls on the event of the resurrection. If Jesus did not rise from the dead, then Christianity is a myth, and we may as well forget it. But the Christian faith does

7

not stand or fall on the evidence for the resurrection. There are many real events in history for which the historical evidence is slim or nonexistent (in fact, when you think about it, most events in history are of this character). But they did actually happen. We just have no way of proving that they happened. Thus, it is entirely conceivable that the resurrection of Jesus was a real event of history, but there is no way of proving this historically. I think that in fact the historical evidence for Jesus' resurrection is good—remarkably good. But that evidence is not the basis of the Christian faith. Should the evidence be refuted somehow, the Christian faith would not be refuted. It would only mean that one could not prove historically that the Christian faith is true.

In point of fact we can know that Jesus rose from the dead wholly apart from a consideration of the historical evidence. The simplest Christian, who has neither the opportunity nor where-withal to conduct a historical investigation of Jesus' resurrection, can know with assurance that Jesus is risen because God's Spirit bears unmistakable witness to him that it is so. And any non-Christian who is truly seeking to know the truth about God and life can also be sure that Jesus is risen because God's Spirit will lead him to a personal relationship with the risen Lord. Thus, there are really two avenues to a knowledge of the fact of the resurrection: the avenue of the Spirit and the avenue of historical inquiry. The former provides a spiritual certainty of the resurrection, whereas the latter provides a rational certainty of the resurrection. Ideally these ought to coincide, the Spirit working through the rational power of the evidence and the evidence undergirding the witness of the Spirit. But even if the historical avenue proved inaccessible, the avenue of the Spirit to a knowledge of the resurrection would remain open and independent.

Thus no one is justified in rejecting the Christian faith simply because "the evidence isn't good enough." If the evidence for the resurrection is inadequate, then we cannot *prove* the resurrection to be an event of history. But God's Spirit still furnishes the unmistakable conviction that the resurrection occurred and that Jesus lives today. Therefore, whatever the state of the evidence, we can be sure that the resurrection is an event of history. Ultimately then, we must come to grips, not with historical evidence, important as this may be, but with the living Lord Himself.

WILLIAM LANE CRAIG
Erlangen, West Germany

1

Death and Resurrection

Man, writes Loren Eiseley, is the Cosmic Orphan.[1] He is the only creature in the universe who asks, Why? Other animals are guided by instincts, but man has learned to ask questions. That is why he is an orphan.

For many centuries man believed that the universe was created by God and that He had placed man on the Earth. But this world view broke apart like an ill-nailed raft caught in a torrent. Space, which had been thought to be a small and homey place for man, suddenly widened into infinity. The earth was seen to be a mere speck drifting in the wake of a minor star, itself rotating around an immense galaxy composed of innumerable suns. Beyond and beyond, billions of light years away, other galaxies vast and innumerable glowed through clouds of wandering gas and interstellar dust. Man finally knew that he was alone in the indifferent immensity of the universe.

"Who am I?" the Orphan cried. And science answered back,

> You are a changeling. You are linked by a genetic chain to all the vertebrates. The thing that is you bears the still aching wounds of evolution in body and in brain. Your hands are made-over fins, your lungs come from a creature gasping in a swamp, your femur has been twisted upright. Your foot is a reworked climbing pad. You are a rag doll resewn from the skins of extinct animals. Long ago, 2,000,000 years perhaps, you were smaller, your brain was not so large. We are not confident that you could speak. Seventy million years before that you were an even smaller climbing creature known as a tupaiid. You were the size of a rat. You ate insects. Now you fly to the Moon.[2]

As the Cosmic Orphan looked to his past he saw only the purposeless, blind processes of mutation and natural selec-

9

tion. Now as he looks to his future, he sees—death. Eiseley relates how this reality was brought home to him as a youth:

When I was a young lad of that indefinite but important age when one begins to ask, Who am I? Why am I here? What is the nature of my kind? What is growing up? What is the world? How long shall I live in it? Where shall I go? I found myself walking with a small companion over a high railroad trestle that spanned a stream, a country bridge, and a road. One could look fearfully down, between the ties, at the shallows and ripples in the shining water some 50 feet below. One was also doing a forbidden thing, against which our parents constantly warned. One must not be caught on the black bridge by a train. Something terrible might happen, a thing called death.

From the abutment of the bridge we gazed down upon the water and saw among the pebbles the shape of an animal we knew only from picture books—a turtle, a very large, dark mahogany-coloured turtle. We scrambled down the embankment to observe him more closely. From the little bridge a few feet above the stream, I saw that the turtle, whose beautiful markings shone in the afternoon sun, was not alive and that his flippers waved aimlessly in the rushing water. The reason for his death was plain. Not too long before we had come upon the trestle, someone engaged in idle practice with a repeating rifle had stitched a row of bullet holes across the turtle's carapace and sauntered on.

My father had once explained to me that it took a long time to make a big turtle, years really, in the sunlight and the water and the mud. I turned the ancient creature over and fingered the etched shell with its forlorn flippers flopping grotesquely. The question rose up unbidden. Why did the man have to kill something living that could never be replaced? I laid the turtle down in the water and gave it a little shove. It entered the current and began to drift away. 'Let's go home,' I said to my companion. From that moment I think I began to grow up.[3]

Eiseley's beautiful and melancholy prose describes poignantly the predicament of modern man. Lost in a universe without God, he is truly the Cosmic Orphan. He was thrown into life as an accidental product of nature, and he faces inevitable extinction in death. His lot is only made more bitter and more tragic by the fact that he of all creatures is aware of it.

But the reason modern man is an orphan is not simply, as Eiseley intimates, because man is a product of evolution or because he asks, Why? It is not even because he is doomed to die. *Modern man is an orphan because he has lost God.* An orphan is a child without parents. If God existed, then even if He created man by means of evolution, man would still be His child. If His child asked, "Why?" there would be an answer in God. Even if man's life ended at the grave, God would still be man's parent.

Modern man is the Cosmic Orphan because he has killed God. And, by doing so, he has reduced himself to an accident of nature. When he asks, Why? his cry is lost in the silence of the recesses of space. When he dies, he dies without hope. Thus, in killing God, modern man has killed himself as well.

It is the absence of God that ultimately makes man the Cosmic Orphan. It is the grim finality of death that makes his life a tragedy. Even if God did exist and had created man, it would still be a tragedy if a personal being like man should have no better fate than to be forever extinguished in death. Death is certainly man's greatest enemy. In losing God, modern man has lost immortality as well. Death means eternal annihilation. This prospect robs life of its meaning and fullness. It makes the life of man no better than the life of a cow or horse, only more tragic. In light of death, the activities that cram our life seem so pointless. Thus Archibald MacLeish described the life of man as an idiotic circus—until one day the show is all over:

> Quite unexpectedly as Vasserot
> The armless ambidextrian was lighting
> A match between his great and second toe
> And Ralph the lion was engaged in biting
> The neck of Madame Sossman while the drum
> Pointed, and Teeny was about to cough

In waltz-time swinging Jocko by the thumb—
Quite unexpectedly the top blew off:

And there, there overhead, there, there, hung over
Those thousands of white faces, those dazed eyes,
There in the starless dark the poise, the hover,
There with vast wings across the canceled skies,
There in the sudden blackness the black pall
Of nothing, nothing, nothing—nothing at all.
                                    "The End of the World"

Herein lies the horror of modern man: because he ultimately ends in nothing, he *is* nothing. The playwright Samuel Beckett also understands this. In his play *Waiting for Godot*, two men carry on trivial conversation for the entire duration of the play while waiting for a third man to arrive. But he never comes. Our lives are like that, Beckett is saying. We just kill time, waiting—for nothing. In another tragic portrayal of the life of man, Beckett opens the curtain to reveal a stage littered with junk. For several long seconds, the audience stares in silence at that junk. Then the curtain closes. That is all.

If there is no immortality, then the life that man does have becomes absurd. To make the situation worse, life is itself only a mixed blessing, for at least four reasons.

First, there is the evil in the heart of man, which expresses itself in man's terrible inhumanity to man. Many people wonder how God could create a world with so much evil in it. But they seem to overlook the fact that most of that evil is the result of man's free choices. War, torture, theft, rape, jealousy, and a thousand other sins are man's own actions. Prior to the twentieth century, people tended to be optimistic about man. The popular slogan was "Every day in every way I am getting better and better." Around the turn of the century a liberal theological magazine called *The Christian Century* was founded. That is what they thought the twentieth century would be. Then came World War I—and then World War II. No longer could man portray himself as an innocent child. Something was radically wrong with him. This conviction is powerfully displayed in Joseph Conrad's novel *The Heart of Darkness*. The title of the novel refers, not to the heart of deepest Africa, where the story takes place, but to the heart of man himself. As the dying man in the story looks into his own heart, his last words are, "The horror! The horror!"

The title of William Golding's novel *The Lord of the Flies* also contains a deep truth about man's nature. For "lord of the flies" is the translation of the ancient word *Baal-zebub*, one of the names of Satan in the New Testament. In Golding's gripping tale, a planeload of English schoolboys marooned on an island degenerates into murderous savages. Golding shows that the evils of society at large stem from the heart of man himself, which is under the domination of the lord of the flies. Perhaps the predicament of modern man was best summarized by G. K. Chesterton in a letter to the London *Times*, which had invited people to write on the subject "What's wrong with the world?" Chesterton answered, "Dear Sirs, I am. Yours truly, G. K. Chesterton." The evil is in man himself. Man's only answer to this problem is to try to program evil out of man by behavioral conditioning. But he thereby reduces man to the level of a laboratory rat, coaxed into the programmer's behavior pattern by rewards and punishments.

Second, there is the problem of disease. Modern man lives in constant fear of killers like cancer, heart disease, and leukemia. You probably have loved ones or friends who have been taken or incapacitated by such diseases, for which no sure cure has been discovered. And what of those born physically deformed or mentally retarded? Is there no release for them? With no hope of immortality, life is often painful and ugly because of such scourges.

Third, all of us confront the specter of aging. Old age is inevitable—unless we die young. It often brings feebleness of body and mind. A visit to a geriatric home where so many elderly are cast away and forgotten can be very depressing. I am saddened by films that depict the life story of a hero from his youth to his old age or death. By condensing the hero's life into the space of a couple of hours, the film brings home to us the fleeting nature of life. The contrast between the vigor of youth and the feebleness of old age is often shattering. If man is not immortal, that is all he can look forward to. Is it no wonder that the elderly are often brushed aside, since they remind us so powerfully of our future and of the transitoriness of life?

Fourth, there is death itself, the great and cruel Joker who cuts down all men, often unexpectedly in the prime of life. Bertrand Russell once remarked that no one can sit by the bedside of a dying child and still believe in God. But when I was in Paris, I met a young American minister who had been trained in seminary and worked in counseling dying children. *What would Bertrand Russell have said to those children?* I wondered. What *could* he say? Too bad? The cruelty would be unimaginable. If there is no immortality, then the capriciousness of death is a tyranny of the bitterest sort.

Confined to this life alone, modern man is set upon by the pressures of life and plagued by his own evil, disease, old age, and ultimately death itself. Historian Stewart C. Easton concludes,

> Thus man is penned within his earthly world; his life began with a birth before which there was nothing and will end with a death after which there is nothing. . . .
>
> Death marks the end of all the life he will ever know; and though there may not be much left to enjoy on earth, it is better than nothing. . . .
>
> Thus modern man is hag-ridden by fear and worry, in spite of all the pleasures that his society through its ingenuity and industry provide him.[4]

Thus, truly, modern man in killing God has unwittingly killed himself as well.

Eiseley does not seem to realize the depth of this tragedy. He seems to regard man's quest for scientific knowledge as somehow providing significance and value to man's life. When the Orphan cries, "Why?" it is *science* who answers back. Science has itself become a sort of religion. Its high priests are the scientists, who speak with the authoritative word to man's questions. But this will never do. Without God, science itself becomes meaningless. Man's search to understand himself and the universe is ultimately without significance. Nor can scientific knowledge provide man with moral values. Eiseley is shocked at the horrors of Auschwitz and Dachau. But if there is no God, then no moral standard exists to condemn such acts. Nor can science overcome the absurdity of life caused by death. Science cannot prolong life forever. It is noteworthy that Eiseley never returns to the question of death, which was awakened in him as a child, to show how science answers this problem. For it cannot. The religion of science has no answer to man's deepest questions.

The point is that man's being the Cosmic Orphan is not an exhilirating adventure. It is the final tragedy. It means that man is the purposeless outcome of matter, time, and chance. He is no more significant than any other animal, and is destined only to die. Therefore we weep for him.

What makes his predicament doubly tragic is that man is in a certain sense naturally oriented toward God and immortality.[5] For man alone possesses what anthropologists call "openness to the world." This means that man is not totally determined by his environment; rather he is free and can create new possibilities that are not immediately at hand in nature. Animals do not have this openness to the world. They do not perceive their environment as fully as man does, but fix their attention on their immediate surroundings. They are also bound to the world by their innate instincts, or drives, which determine how they will perceive the world and how they will act. But in man innate instincts are not so specialized or strong. He can think about the options confronting him and create new alternatives. He considers the whole world, which for him is not just an environment. In fact, man is open beyond the world. Every level he reaches, he surpasses. He strives beyond every finite level towards an unknown goal. Man is oriented toward the infinite, for any lesser goal would not satisfy his endless striving. In this sense, man is oriented toward God. Only in the infinite being of God can man's fundamental striving be fulfilled. I am reminded of Augustine's words, "You have made us for Yourself, O God, and our hearts are restless till they find their rest in You."

But not only is man oriented toward God—he is also oriented toward immortality. Only man considers and anticipates the future. Animals live only in the present, but man in his expectations, his fantasies, his dreams looks to the future. He hopes that even if he is not happy now—well, tomorrow may bring better things. But this consciousness of the future brings with it a terrible drawback. He alone, among all living creatures, anticipates his death. This results in an odd paradox: man hopes for the future, yet at the same time he knows that the future brings death one step closer. This paradox suggests that just as it belongs to man's nature to know of his own coming death, so it belongs to his nature to hope for life beyond death. The hope for immortality thus seems to be as peculiarly characteristic of man as his orientation toward God.

But if there is no God or immortality, then not only is man a Cosmic Orphan, thrown into existence without purpose; he is also the victim of a colossal and cruel joke. His thirst for those realities that he so desperately needs to give significance and value to his life, but which he tragically lacks, is built into his very nature as man. God and immortality—the very realities toward which man is oriented—are precisely the realities that do not exist. The predicament of modern man is not simply that he is an orphan, but that he is an orphan oriented by nature toward the very things he needs but cannot have.

Our Options

What are we to do in this predicament? As I see it, there are four options.

1. *Commit suicide.* Faced with the absurdity and meanness of life, one ought simply to end it now. This is not so outlandish as it sounds. The French writer Albert Camus considered suicide to be the only serious philosophic question. Is it worthwhile to go on living? Hamlet asked the same question when he mused, "To be or not to be; that is the question." Occasionally one hears of persons who answer Hamlet's question in the negative. The student riots in France in 1968, for example, were triggered when one young man, fed up with his materialistic society, walked into the basement of a university building and hanged himself in protest. But most of us would answer the question as Hamlet did: suicide is not worth it. The fear of the unknown and the pleasures that life does afford constrain us to go on living.

2. *Ignore the whole thing.* Use any number of escape mechanisms to avoid asking the question of the meaning of life. Easton comments on modern man's means of escape:

> It is easier to sink into an intellectual sloth, to put aside, if he can, his worries, and either be entertained or undertake a mindless escape in the many ways provided for him by an industrial economy—drugging the mind with alcohol, speeding over the highways and waterways, talking idly with friends and acquaintances, pursuing a golf ball in an electrically propelled cart and occasionally exercising his muscles by hitting it. Then the persistent thought that he is a human being and that he is not developing all his human potentialities will not come up to plague him.[6]

And do not think this escapism is confined to the bourgeois middle class. The student generation also tries to escape—through drugs. Drug taking may not be an ideology anymore, but it is still a popular escapism. It is simple to blow your mind on acid rock and marijuana in the privacy of your own dorm room.

The problem with this option, however, is twofold. First, it cannot bring man fulfillment in life. Easton remarks, "It remains incontestable that the simple pursuit of his various forms of enjoyment does not lead to happiness, but leaves him both sated and dissatisfied."[7] Second, the risks involved in ignoring the problem are too great. For what if God does exist and life does have meaning? One runs the risk of losing everything by avoiding this question. Socrates said the unexamined life is not worth living. That is doubly true when the question is the existence of God and life after death. The question takes on added urgency because death's grinning face threatens to meet us around every turn, when we least expect it.

The great Russian author Leo Tolstoy exclaimed, "Death, death, death! Your whole life passes in the presence of death!" Yet he points out in his story *The Death of Ivan Illyitch* that we always think of death in terms of the *other* person— never ourselves. Then suddenly it is too late. Anglican minister David C. K. Watson reports, "As a minister I am constantly visiting bereaved people, and I find that the outstanding reaction is always that of shock. Death, although vaguely expected at some future time, nearly always takes the relatives by surprise."[8] "Yet," he continues, "we have so many vivid and personal reminders of the shortness of life and the suddenness of death." Probably all of us know of friends or relatives who have been unexpectedly cut down by accidents or disease. The question of God is too important to put off until it is too late.

3. *Affirm the absurdity of life and live nobly.* I think this option has a certain appeal. Here we get the picture of the noble humanist who recognizes his situation but laughs in the face of it. As he walks unblindfolded to the gallows, his step is unfaltering. He lives bravely and dedicates himself to the service of his fellow man. He needs no God, as weaker people do, for he is the captain of his soul. He is a freethinker. No antiquated morality prevents him from acting as he wishes. His only standard is love for his fellowman.

But there are two things disastrously wrong with this stance. First, it is totally inconsistent. If there is no God, then neither oneself nor one's fellowman has any value. As

Easton states, "There is no objective reason why he should be moral, unless morality 'pays off' in his social life, or . . . makes him 'feel good.' There is no objective reason why man should do anything save for the pleasure it affords him."[9] It is impossible to found a humanist morality on an atheistic philosophy. It is very doubtful whether any atheist has ever lived consistently with his philosophy.

But second, it is a noble picture only if there is no God or immortality. If there *is* a God and immortality, then the humanist is not brave, noble, or strong—he is pathetic, pitiful, and deluded. He is like the man who stood up in Hyde Park Corner in London and said, "People tell me that God exists; but I can't see him! People tell me there is life after death; but I can't see it! People tell me there is a heaven and hell; but I can't see them!" After he had finished, another man struggled onto the soap box. He began, "People tell me that there is green grass around us; but I can't see it. People tell me there are trees nearby; but I can't see them. People tell me there is a blue sky above; but I can't see it. You see, . . . I'm blind."[10] If there is a God and immortality, then the humanist is not the noble figure he paints himself to be; rather he is blind and rebellious toward God.

And who is to say that there is no God or immortality? Humanists just seem to take it for granted. The fact is, no philosopher has ever been able to construct a sound disproof of the existence of God. And science cannot disprove God either, since it deals only with physical realities. The religion of science glorifies one aspect of reality as though it were the whole of reality. Neither biology nor astronomy disproves God. God could have used evolution as His means of creating man; indeed, the notion that a tree shrew evolved by *chance* to a personal being who journeys to the moon appears at face value rather preposterous. And astronomy in demonstrating that the universe had a beginning a finite number of years ago (about 9 billion according to a recent estimate) actually points to the existence of a Creator of the universe. So how can humanists be so sure that there is no

God or immortality? I suspect that it is because they simply do not want God to exist, since that would mean that they are not, after all, the captains of their souls.

4. *Challenge the world view of modern man.* If it is affirmed that there is a God and immortality, then man is not the Cosmic Orphan after all. Life has significance and value. Modern man has no proof that God and immortality are illusions. So could they not in fact be realities? That is the position of biblical Christianity. It affirms that a personal Creator God does exist. It also affirms personal immortality for man. This is the wonderful promise that it holds out to man: "For God so loved the world, that He gave His only begotten Son, that whoever believes in Him should not perish, but have eternal life" (John 3:16).

But it is important to understand what sort of immortality the Bible affirms. Biblical Christianity teaches immortality in the form of *resurrection from the dead*. Jesus said, "For this is the will of My Father, that every one who beholds the Son, and believes in Him, may have eternal life; and I Myself will raise him up on the last day" (John 6:40). We need to define this notion of resurrection more closely.

First, resurrection is not the immortality of the soul alone. The view of ancient Greek philosophy was that the body is the prison of the soul. When the body dies, the soul is at last released from its bondage to dwell in heaven. By contrast, the biblical view is that the body is good and is an integral part of man. Though the soul can exist without the body, it is in such a state incomplete and a mere shadow of what a fully human person is. To be a man is to be a body and soul in unity.

Second, resurrection is not reincarnation. The doctrine of reincarnation is found in certain Eastern religions. Reincarnation is considered a curse, not a blessing. The evil that one experiences in this life is the punishment for his soul's behavior in a previous life. If one does not act properly in this life, his soul is sentenced to live yet another life after this one. The goal is actually to escape reincarnation so that the soul returns to the World Soul like a drop of water to the ocean. Thus, the real goal is personal annihilation. By contrast, the biblical view is that a man lives only one lifetime and then is raised from the dead and judged by God. Thus, resurrection stands diametrically opposed to reincarnation.

Third, resurrection is not resuscitation. The mere bringing back of a corpse to life is not a resurrection. For a person who has resuscitated returns only to this earthly life and will die again. By contrast, resurrection is to eternal life, and a person raised from the dead is immortal.

Finally, resurrection is not translation. The Jews had a view called translation, which was the immediate assumption of a man directly into heaven. Death was not a condition for translation; a living man might be taken directly into heaven. By contrast, resurrection is not a direct assumption of someone into heaven; rather it is the raising up of the dead man in the space-time universe. Death is always a precondition, and the resurrected man is still part of the created world.

The biblical view of immortality is that at history's end, when God brings about the end of the world, He will raise up all those who have died and so reconstitute them as whole men of body and soul in union. Then they will be judged, and their eternal destiny determined.

Now the question is, Which, if any of these views of life and death is correct? If we could wait until history's end, then we could see if the biblical view of resurrection is indeed true. But by then it would be too late. Fortunately, in this case, however, we have a very peculiar circumstance that allows us to determine now the truth of the biblical doctrine of resurrection; namely, the biblical conviction that a man has been raised from the dead by God *in advance* as the basis and pattern for our future resurrection. That man was, of course, Jesus of Nazareth. If the historical evidence is sufficient to indicate that He did in fact rise from the dead, then we have sufficient grounds for affirming the truth of the biblical view.

Thus, the historicity of the resurrection of Jesus becomes

of paramount importance to modern man. If it is true, then the Cosmic Orphan has found his home; for the resurrection of Jesus gives him both God and immortality at once. If it is not true, then he lapses back into his lonely search. Therefore, the paramount question that we must now address is: Did Jesus of Nazareth really rise from the dead?

NOTES

1. *Encyclopaedia Britannica*, 15th ed., *Propaedia*, s.v. "The cosmic orphan," by Loren Eiseley.
2. Ibid.
3. Ibid.
4. Stewart C. Easton, *The Western Heritage*, 2d ed. (New York: Holt, Rinehart & Winston, 1966), p. 878.
5. See Wolfhart Pannenberg, *Was ist der Mensch? Die Anthropologie der Gegenwart im Lichte der Theologie* (Göttingen: Vandenhoeck & Ruprecht, 1962), pp. 6-11, 31-33.
6. Easton, *Heritage*, p. 877.
7. Ibid., p. 878.
8. David C. K. Watson, *My God Is Real* (New York: Seabury, 1970), p. 41.
9. Easton, *Heritage*, p. 878.
10. A story related by Watson, *God*, p. 80.

2

Some Blind Alleys

Ever since the disciples began to proclaim that Jesus was risen from the dead, some have denied the historical resurrection and have tried to come up with ways of explaining away the evidence through alternative theories. Most of these alternative explanations have proved to be blind alleys and have been unanimously rejected by contemporary scholarship.

Nevertheless, a review of some of these theories of the past is useful, primarily for two reasons. First, the average person today, Christian or non-Christian, is largely unaware that they are in fact blind alleys. Many non-Christians still reject or at least claim to reject Jesus' resurrection because of arguments that have been decisively refuted time and again and which no modern scholar would support. And Christians often produce arguments for the resurrection that are aimed at eighteenth-century opponents and cannot therefore really come to grips with modern skepticism. It is important therefore to discover exactly what these dead ends are so that we need not be unnecessarily sidetracked by them in the future. Second, an examination of now passé theories and the grounds for rejecting them will help to clear the ground for our discussion in the upcoming chapters. We will be able to focus our attention on the evidence for the resurrection and deal with the real issues of modern criticism. Therefore, it is very important indeed to see what issues are now obsolete and what issues are important today.

THE CONSPIRACY THEORY

We find the very first alternative explanation to Jesus' resurrection in the pages of the New Testament itself: *the conspiracy theory*. In Matthew's gospel we discover that the

23

Jews used this theory to explain away the resurrection. The chief priests bribed the guards who were at Jesus' tomb, instructing them: "You are to say 'His disciples came by night and stole Him away while we were asleep.' . . . And they took the money and did as they had been instructed; and this story was widely spread among the Jews, and is to this day" (Matthew 28:13, 15). This rumor must have been fairly current among the Jews at that time, or Matthew would not have felt obligated to expose it. The conspiracy theory was thus the first alternative to the resurrection of Jesus and held basically that the resurrection was a hoax: the disciples stole the body and then lied about Jesus' appearances to them afterwards.

The conspiracy theory was refuted by the early church historian Eusebius of Caesarea in his *Demonstratio evangelica* (314-18).[1] Eusebius argues that it would be inconsistent to hold that the disciples were on one hand followers of Jesus with His high moral teaching and yet on the other hand such base liars as to invent all these miraculous stories about Jesus. It makes no sense to say that the men who learned and then taught the ethics of Jesus would themselves be deceivers.

Not only that, Eusebius continues, but it is inconceivable that such a conspiracy could ever be formed or hold together. Eusebius composes a wonderfully satirical speech, which he imagines to have been delivered when the disciples first joined together in this conspiracy.

"Let us band together," the speaker proclaims, "to invent all the miracles and resurrection appearances which we never saw and let us carry the sham even to death! Why not die for nothing? Why dislike torture and whipping inflicted for no good reason? Let us go out to all nations and overthrow their institutions and denounce their gods! And even if we don't convince anybody, at least we'll have the satisfaction of drawing down on ourselves the punishment for our own deceit."

Through this satire, Eusebius wants to show how

ridiculous it is to imagine that the disciples invented the whole thing. But even if they had, he continues, the plot would never have held together. How could so many persons agree unanimously to lie about these things? Could such an enterprise engineered by liars ever endure? Eusebius points out that these men went to their deaths testifying to the truth of what they believed. It is unbelievable that they would suffer and die for nothing. And how could the testimonies of all these deceivers agree? The disciples gave up family, worldly pleasures, and money to go out into foreign lands to preach what they believed. They could not have been liars. Eusebius, himself a great historian, emphasizes that if we distrust these men, then we must distrust all writers of history and records. If we accept the testimony of secular historians, then we must by the same standard also accept the reliability of the disciples' testimony to the resurrection.

The theory of conspiracy by the disciples surfaced again in the seventeenth and eighteenth centuries, being supported this time by the deists. The deists believed in God, but they denied that God ever acted in the world. He just sort of wound up the world like a clock, set it ticking, and let it go on its own. H. S. Reimarus (d. 1769) held that Jesus had tried to establish an earthly kingdom but failed and was executed. The disciples enjoyed the easy life of preaching the gospel, so they stole Jesus' body and proclaimed that Jesus was a purely spiritual king with a future coming kingdom.[2]

The attacks of the deists brought forth a flood of books on the historical evidences for Jesus' miracles and resurrection. That was one of the most fruitful periods in the history of Christian literature on evidences for the truth of the Christian faith. To name just one example, Nathaniel Lardner's *The Credibility of the Gospel History* (1730-55), the result of a lifetime of research, consists of twelve volumes and is an impressive work by any standard. The Christian thinkers absolutely steamrollered the deists' objections into the ground. After the eighteenth century, the conspiracy theory was laid permanently to rest and never again gained the consensus of scholarship. Let us summarize some of the main arguments used by the Christians in refuting this theory:

1. The obvious sincerity of the disciples is evident in their suffering and dying for what they believed. The Christian thinkers here picked up Eusebius's argument. To charge the disciples with a cheap hoax flies in the face of their all too apparent sincerity. It is impossible to deny that the disciples honestly believed that Jesus had risen from the dead, in light of their life of suffering and their dying for this truth. Reimarus's contention that the disciples made this up so they could continue their "easy life" of preaching is nothing but a poor joke.

2. The disciples' moral character proves that they were not liars. They were men of unquestioned moral uprightness and clearly sincere about what they said. They were also simple, ordinary people, not cunning deceivers. Moreover, they had absolutely nothing of worldly value to gain by preaching this doctrine—but they had a great deal to lose. So why should we not believe that they were telling the truth?

3. The idea of a conspiracy is ridiculous. It is just inconceivable that one of the disciples would suggest to his fellow disciples that they steal Jesus' body and say that he had risen when he and they knew that to be false. How could he possibly rally his bewildered friends into such a project? And are we then to think they would all stand confidently before judges declaring the truth of this figment of their imaginations? Besides that, common experience shows that such conspiracies inevitably unravel; either someone breaks down or slips up or the affair is otherwise discovered by opponents, in this case the Jews. The disciples, even if had they wanted to, could never have pulled off a conspiracy of such unmanageable proportions.

4. The gospels were written soon after the events and in the same place where the events had happened. Thus it

would have been almost impossible for them to be lies. The disciples preached the resurrection in Jerusalem in the face of their enemies only a few weeks after Jesus was crucified. Under such circumstances, the disciples could never have preached the resurrection if it had not occurred.

5. The disciples could not have stolen the body from the tomb, had they wanted to. The Jews had set the guard around the tomb specifically to prevent theft of the corpse. The story that the disciples stole the body while the guard slept is ridiculous, for (a) how could the guards have known that it was the disciples who stole the body, if they had been sleeping? And (b) it is ludicrous to imagine the disciples' breaking into the sealed tomb and carting away the body while the guards were peacefully sleeping at the very door. Thus, the theft hypothesis is hopelessly impossible.

6. The change in the disciples shows they had not invented the resurrection. After the crucifixion the disciples were confused, defeated, fearful, and burdened with sorrow. Suddenly they changed, becoming fearless preachers of Jesus' resurrection. They suffered bravely and confidently for this fact. They went from the depths of despair to the boldest certainty. This incredible change in the disciples showed that they were not merely lying, but were absolutely convinced that Jesus had risen from the dead.

7. The disciples became convinced of the resurrection despite every skeptical doubt and every predisposition to the contrary. They had been reared in a religion (Judaism) that was vastly different from what they later preached. They had in particular no inkling whatsoever that the Jewish Messiah (the prophesied coming King of Israel) would die and rise from the dead. When the women found the empty tomb, the disciples did not believe them. When Jesus appeared to them, they thought they were seeing a ghost. They were not at all inclined to believe in Jesus' resurrection, but were convinced almost in spite of themselves.

In summary, the deist who holds to this theory must believe (1) that twelve poor fishermen were able to change the world through a plot laid so deep that no one has ever been able to discern where the cheat lay, (2) that these men gave up the pursuit of happiness and ventured into poverty, torments, and persecutions for nothing, (3) that depressed and fearful men would have suddenly grown so brave as to break into the tomb and steal the body, and (4) that these imposters would furnish the world with the greatest system of morality that ever was.

The high point of the Christian response to the attacks of the deists came with William Paley's *A View of the Evidences of Christianity* (1794),[3] a work so successful that it remained compulsory reading for any applicant to Cambridge University right up until the twentieth century. It is worthwhile to survey briefly Paley's arguments, for not only do they deal a death blow to the deistical objections, but many of his arguments have force against modern objections to the resurrection as well.

Paley's positive case for the Christian faith consists in his defense of two statements: (1) that the original witnesses of Christian miracles voluntarily passed their lives in labor and suffering for the truth of what they proclaimed and that they also for the same reason adopted a new way of life, and (2) that no similar case exists in history. In support of the first point, Paley argues that (a) Jesus and the disciples did what the statement says, and (b) they did it because of the miraculous story found in the gospels.

In support of subpoint (a), Paley first argues from the general nature of the case. We know that the Christian faith exists. Either it was founded by Jesus and the disciples or it was founded later by others, the first being silent. But it is unbelievable that it could have been founded by others, if Jesus and the disciples did and said nothing. If the disciples had not zealously followed up what Jesus had started, Christianity would have died at its birth. If this is correct, then the first disciples must have been involved in missionary activity. Such a life, Paley points out, is not without its own sort of enjoyment, but it is an enjoyment that springs only from a true sincerity. With the consciousness at bottom of hollowness and faslehood, the fatigue and strain would have become unbearable.

Moreover, there was probably difficulty and danger involved in spreading a new faith. The Jews would oppose it because the idea of Jesus' being the Messiah was contrary to Jewish expectations and because the disciples could not avoid implicitly accusing the Jewish leadership of an unjust and cruel murder. The pagan religions would not be sympathetic to the Christian faith either, since Christians did not acknowledge the existence of any other god. So even if there were no widespread program of persecution, random outbursts of violence against Christians probably occurred.

Finally, the very nature of the case requires that these early gospel preachers must have experienced a great change in their lives. For now they were involved in preaching, prayer, religious meetings, and teaching new converts.

What one would expect from the general nature of the case is, in fact, precisely what history tells us actually happened. The Roman historian Tacitus relates the persecution by Nero about thirty years after Jesus' death, when Christians were smeared with pitch and used as human torches to illuminate the night, while Nero rode about Rome in the costume of a charioteer, viewing the spectacle. The testimonies of the Roman authors Seutonius and Juvenal confirm that within thirty-one years after Jesus' death, Christians were dying for their faith. From the writings of Pliny the Younger, Martial, Epictetus, and Marcus Aurelius, it is clear that the believers voluntarily submitted to torture and death rather than renounce their faith. That suffering is often mentioned in Christian writings as well. For example, Jesus' predictions that His followers would be persecuted were either real predictions come true or else were put back into His mouth because persecution had come about. Either way, it shows that Christians were suffering for their faith. In the book of Acts in the New Testament, the believers' suffering is described soberly and without extravagance. The letters in the New Testament abound with references to persecution and with commands to hold fast. The early Christian writers, Clement, Hermas, Polycarp, and Ignatius mention the sufferings that the Christians were undergoing. They also bear witness that the Christian believers had adopted a new way of life.

As for subpoint (b), it is equally clear that those early Christians were suffering for a *miraculous* story. The gospel story is a story of miracles, and we have no other story than the one contained in the gospels. The early letters of Barnabas and Clement refer to Jesus' miracles and resurrection. Polycarp mentions the resurrection of Jesus, and Irenaeus writes that as a young man he had heard Polycarp tell of Jesus' miracles. Ignatius mentions the resurrection. Quadratus reports that people were still living who had been healed by Jesus. Justin Martyr refers to the miracles of Jesus. *No trace of a nonmiraculous story exists.* That an original nonmiraculous story should be completely lost and another miraculous story replace it goes beyond any known example of corruption of even oral tradition, not to speak of written historical transmission. The gospels themselves indicate that the story they were telling was not their own invention, but that it was already widely known and told.

Thus, it is clear that the miraculous story in the gospels was the story which the Christian believers had from the beginning. This means that the resurrection of Jesus was always a part of that story. Were we to stop here, says Paley, we would have a situation unparalleled in history: that during the reign of Tiberius Caesar certain persons began a new religious faith and that in so doing they voluntarily submitted to great dangers, suffering, and labor, all for a miraculous story that they proclaimed wherever they went, and that the resurrection of a dead man whom they had known well was an integral part of that story.

But we need not stop here, continues Paley. We should rather now ask, Were the gospels really written by Matthew, Mark, Luke, and John? If even one gospel can be shown to be genuine, then that will be enough to ensure the truth of the story.

Paley suggests several considerations that all point to

the authenticity of the gospels. The apostles, he argues, would eventually have needed to publish accurate accounts of Jesus' life and ministry, in which case any false gospels would be discredited and the genuine gospels preserved. Also the agreement between the four gospels, even when common sources behind them are acknowledged, and between the gospels and the New Testament letters shows that the story is historically trustworthy. The Hebrew and Syriac expressions in the gospels are what we would expect from the authors usually assigned to the gospels. If it were so easy to produce works under false names, then we would have more forged writings attributed to Jesus Himself. There was widespread early agreement that the gospels were genuine writings of their commonly accepted authors. In fact, Paley remarks, there is no more reason to doubt that the gospels were written by Matthew, Mark, Luke, and John than there is to doubt that the works of secular authors like Philo or Josephus come from their authors. The only reason skeptics doubt the gospels' authenticity is that it is a miraculous story, and skeptics simply refuse to accept miracles.

All of the above considerations are important, states Paley. But the strongest argument that the gospels are genuine writings of their authors is ancient testimony to that fact. Here Paley expounds an elaborate eleven-point argument:

1. The gospels and Acts are quoted as genuine by ancient writers, beginning with those from the time of the apostles themselves and continuing thereafter. This sort of proof is the strongest argument for the authenticity of a writing and is regularly used by ordinary historians to prove that a particular work came from a certain author. This method, when applied to the gospels and Acts, establishes without question their authenticity. For example, the Epistle of Barnabas quotes Matthew as Scripture, and Clement of Rome also quotes words of Jesus found in Matthew. The Shepherd of Hermas alludes to Matthew, Luke, and John. Ignatius, who was a church leader in Antioch about thirty-seven years

after Christ's death alludes to Matthew and John. His contemporary, Polycarp, who knew personally the disciple John and other eyewitnesses to Jesus' ministry, refers to different New Testament works some forty times. Papias, who also knew John, specifically says Matthew and Mark wrote their gospels; the offhand way in which he makes this remark shows that it was a fact generally known. Justin Martyr about twenty years later frequently quotes the gospels; he does not specify which gospel he is quoting, which shows that the four gospels must have been the only ones in existence at that time. Irenaeus, who knew Polycarp, specifically names the four gospel writers. Paley traces this chain of ancient writers all the way to Eusebius in A.D. 315.

2. The books of the New Testament were always quoted as authoritative and as one of a kind. The ancient writers did not quote them as they would quote any ordinary piece of literature. These books were special and unique and possessed final authority on what they said. Paley provides quotations from Theophilus, the writer against Artemon, Hippolitus, Origen, and many others to prove the point.

3. The books of the New Testament were collected as one volume at a very early date. Today we divide the New Testament into the gospels (the story of Jesus' ministry, death, and resurrection) and the epistles (the letters written by the early apostles like Paul, Peter, and John). The ancient writers made a similar distinction, only they called it the Gospels and the Apostles. Ignatius mentions collections of New Testament books into the Gospels and the Apostles. According to Eusebius, Quadratus distributed the gospels to converts during his travels. Irenaeus and Melito refer to the collection of writings that we today call the New Testament. Clement of Alexandria and Tertullian also refer to the division of Scripture into the Gospels and Apostles. This shows that the gospels were collected together by the early church.

4. These writings were given titles of respect. Polycarp, Justin Martyr, Dionysius, Irenaeus, and others refer to them

as "scriptures," "divine writings," and so forth.

5. These writings were publically read and preached upon. Paley quotes Justin Martyr, Tertullian, Origen, and Cyprian to prove the point.

6. Copies, commentaries, and harmonies of the gospels were written. Thousands upon thousands of copies of the New Testament books were laboriously made by hand. Many commentaries and other works on them were written by men such as Pantaenus, Clement of Alexandria, Tertullian, and so on. It is especially noteworthy that during the first three hundred years, no commentary was written on any book outside the New Testament, with the sole exception of Clement's commentary on the so-called Revelation of Peter. Harmonies, or combinations of the four gospels into one, were also composed, for example, Tatian's Diatessaron (c. A.D. 170).

7. The New Testament books were accepted by all heretical groups as well as by orthodox Christians. Examples of such heretics include Basilides, the Valentinians, the Carpocratians, and many others. Though they all denied some aspect of New Testament teaching, they nevertheless acknowledged the authenticity of the New Testament books themselves.

8. The gospels, Acts, thirteen letters of Paul, 1 John, and 1 Peter were recognized as authentic writings even by those who doubted the authenticity of certain other New Testament epistles. For example, Origen cites the book of Hebrews to support a particular point he is making. He notes that some persons might doubt the authority of Hebrews, but he says that the same point could be proved from the undisputed books of Scripture. He then quotes Matthew and Acts. According to Origen, the four gospels were received without doubt by the whole church of God under heaven. In the same way, Eusebius reports that although some doubted certain epistles, the four gospels were universally recognized as authentic.

9. The early enemies of Christianity recognized that the

gospels contained the story on which the faith was founded. Celsus, for example, admits that the gospels were written by the apostles. Porphyry attacked the Christian faith as it is found in the gospels. The heretic Julian pursued the same procedure.

10. Lists of authentic Scriptures were published, which always included the gospels and Acts. Citations from Origen, Athanasius, Cyril, and others prove the point.

11. The apocryphal books were never treated in the above manner. The apocryphal books were forgeries, which were written in the second century after Christ. They purported to be writings of the apostles and carried titles like the Gospel of Peter, the Gospel of Thomas, and so forth. It is a simple historical fact that during the first three hundred years, with one exception, no apocryphal gospel was ever even quoted by any known writer. In fact, there is no evidence that any forged gospel whatever existed in the first century, during which time the four gospels and Acts were written. The apocryphal gospels were never quoted, never read or preached upon in Christian assemblies, not collected into a volume, not included in the lists of authentic Scriptures, not appealed to by heretics, not noticed by Christianity's enemies, not the subject of commentaries or harmonies, but were nearly universally rejected by Christian writers of that age.

Therefore, Paley concludes, the gospels must be the authentic writings of the apostles. Even if it were the case that the names of the gospel authors were wrong, it still cannot be denied in light of the above arguments that the gospels do contain the story that the original apostles told and for which they labored and suffered. Therefore, the story must be true. The only alternative would be that the apostles were all liars. But that has already been shown to be impossible in light of their sufferings and changed lives. That can only mean that the gospel story must be true.

Paley then turns to his proof of statement (2) that no similar case exists in history. I shall not summarize his argument here in such detail as I did his proof for statement (1). Paley lays down rules that can be used in assessing claims to miracles. He argues that in most cases, the evidence for a genuine miracle is not clear and that the supposed miracles are usually fakes or exaggerations, or are attributable to psychosomatic factors. In those cases where miracles cannot be explained, it still remains true that there is no evidence that the witnesses to those miracles have then voluntarily submitted to labor, danger, and suffering for the truth of the story that they told. Thus, the situation with the disciples and the gospel story of Jesus is without parallel in history.

In the second volume of his masterful work, Paley discusses confirmatory evidence for the truth of the Christian faith, such as fulfilled prophecy, the historical accuracy of the gospels, the excellence of Jesus' moral character, and so on. The chapter that discusses the evidence for the resurrection deserves our attention.

He begins by observing that the whole of the New Testament testifies to the reality of Jesus' resurrection. That leaves us with only two alternatives: the apostles were either deceivers or deceived. The first alternative, that the apostles were deceivers, has been to a large extent abandoned, Paley remarks, because of the obvious sincerity of the disciples, as well as their high moral character and the suffering they endured for the gospel.

The second alternative, that the disciples were deceived, implies that the belief in the resurrection is due to religious hysteria and hallucinations. But this alternative fails on several grounds: (1) Not just one person saw Jesus appear after His resurrection, but many. (2) Not just lone individuals saw Him, but groups of people. (3) They did not see Him only once, but many times. (4) They did not merely see Him, but touched Him, conversed with Him, and ate with Him. (5) Jesus' body was not to be found. That is the decisive argument against the religious hallucination hypothesis. For it is impossible that Jesus' followers could have believed that He was raised from the dead if the corpse were there before them in the tomb. It is equally impossible to suppose that the disciples could have stolen the body and perpetrated a fraud. Moreover, Christianity was founded in Jerusalem. That would have been impossible if Jesus' body were still in the tomb. The Jews would have produced Jesus' corpse as the shortest and completest answer to the whole story. Instead, all they could do was invent the lame excuse that the disciples had stolen the body. Thus, since the hypothesis of religious hallucinations is unable to explain the empty tomb, it ultimately collapses back into the conspiracy theory, which has already been seen to be ridiculous. Therefore, the historical resurrection of Jesus remains the best explanation of the facts.

The arguments of Paley and his predecessors buried the conspiracy theory forever. I cannot emphasize strongly enough that *no modern biblical scholar would for a moment entertain the theory that the disciples conspired together to steal the corpse and then lie about the resurrection appearances.* It is utterly out of the question. The fact that this issue is still batted back and forth at the popular level is sad testimony to the terrible lack of communication between the specialist and the man on the street. The theory has been dead for nearly two hundred years.

The Apparent Death Theory

Another explanation that cropped up after the controversy with the deists was *the apparent death theory*. H. E. G. Paulus in *Das Leben Jesu* (1828) argued that all the miracles recorded in the gospels could be explained by purely natural causes. He was the high-water mark of the natural explanation school and devised all sorts of clever explanations for Jesus' various miracles. As for the resurrection, Paulus held that Jesus did not really die on the cross but was laid unconscious in the tomb. There He revived, managed to escape, and convinced His disciples that He had been raised from the dead. It is an unfortunate note of history that F. D. E. Schleiermacher, the father of modern theology, also adopted this theory.

The theory, however, proved to be as worthless as the conspiracy theory. The natural explanation school as a whole suffered from a brittle artificiality. Paulus's explanations of the miracles of the gospels were themselves so contrived that it was easier to believe in the miracles. His explanation of Jesus' resurrection through a merely apparent death was especially ridiculous:

1. The theory failed to take seriously the extent of Jesus' physical injury. In order to demonstrate this, let us review the events leading up to Jesus' death and burial. Jesus was arrested on a Thursday night and tried illegally by a night session of the Jewish court. During the trial, they spit on Him; they blindfolded Him and hit Him in the face with their fists. They turned Him over to the guards, who beat Him further. Up all night without sleep, Jesus was taken Friday morning to the Roman governor, Pontius Pilate, who in turn sent Him off to the Jewish king, Herod, who after interrogation sent Him back to Pilate. Condemned before a crowd screaming for His blood, Jesus was given to the Roman guards, who whipped Him. They made a crown of thorns and shoved it down onto His head and beat Him with a stick. Jesus was then compelled to carry the heavy cross, on which he was to be crucified, through the streets of the city to the place of crucifixion. Unable to bear the load, He collapsed from exhaustion. Another man was forced to carry the cross the remainder of the way. Jesus was then laid on the cross, and nails were driven though his wrists and a spike through his feet. Judging from skeletal remains of crucifixion victims, this could have been done by first nailing the wrists of the victim to the cross, then twisting the body sideways and driving the spike through both ankles. In this contorted position, the victim was then raised up on the cross, and the cross was dropped into a hole in the ground.

The Shroud of Turin, whether it is the authentic burial cloth of Jesus or not, illustrates graphically the extent of Jesus' physical suffering. The image of the man on the cloth is covered front and back with wounds from head to foot, where the *flagrum*, a multi-thonged Roman whip tipped with metal or bone, had torn apart his flesh, furnishing us a grisly picture of what Jesus must have looked like when He was laid on the cross.

Death by crucifixion is slow and gruesome. As the victim hangs on the cross, his lung cavity collapses, so that he can no longer breathe. In order to breathe, he must pull himself up on those nail-pierced hands and push with his feet until he can catch a breath. But he cannot remain in this position very long. So he has to let himself drop back down. Then he cannot breathe anymore, so he must start the painful ascent all over again, in order to get air. And so it goes, hour after hour after hour, until the victim is too weak to pull himself up and so literally chokes to death. Sometimes the Romans sped up the process by breaking the legs of the victim with a mallet (called in Latin *crurifragum*), so that he could no longer push himself up to breathe, and the victim, dangling helplessly by his arms, died of asphyxiation. It is interesting to note that because it is difficult to determine just when the victim dies, the Romans, if they did not simply leave the body on the cross until the flesh decayed or was eaten by birds or wild animals, would ensure death by stabbing the victim with a lance.[4] The Roman executioners were aware that death might be apparent and had a method of ensuring that the victim was really dead.

The gospels report that although the Roman guards broke the legs of the two men crucified with Jesus, they did not break Jesus' legs because they saw that He was already dead. According to procedure, one of the soldiers took his spear and stabbed Jesus in the side to ensure that He was dead, and, John reports, blood and water flowed out. This flow could have been a serum from the pericardial sac, mixed with blood from the heart, or a hemorrhagic fluid in the pleural cavity between the ribs and the lungs. Jesus was then taken down from the cross and buried in the customary Jewish manner. This included binding the hands and feet and wrapping the body in linen and aromatic spices, in Jesus' case about seventy-five pounds of them. The body was then laid in a tomb carved out of rock, and a great stone was laid across the entrance. This was then sealed, and, according to Matthew, a guard was set around the tomb.

Bearing those facts in mind, we see how foolish the apparent death theory is. Considering the beatings of Jesus, His exhausting all-night trial and interrogations, His scourging, His crucifixion, the spear in His side, the binding and wrapping of the body in seventy-five pounds of linen and spices, and the cold tomb sealed by a large stone, it is just out of the question to suppose that Jesus had not died and had somehow escaped from the tomb to convince His disciples that He had risen from the dead.

2. The apparent-death theory makes Jesus into a deceiver. The necessary implication of the theory is that Jesus was a charlatan who tricked the disciples into believing that He had been raised from the dead. Such a portrait of Jesus is a figment of the imagination. Jesus was one of the world's great moral teachers, a deeply religious man, if nothing else. It is impossible to cast Him in the role of a hoaxer.

3. A weak and half-dead Jesus could never have convinced the disciples that He was the Lord of life and Conqueror of death. D. F. Strauss denied the historical resurrection of Jesus, as we shall see; nevertheless, he rejected Paulus's apparent death theory as completely ridiculous:

> It is impossible that a being who had stolen half-dead out of the sepulchre, who crept about weak and ill, wanting medical treatment, who required bandaging, strengthening and indulgence, and who still at last yielded to his sufferings, could have given to his disciples the impression that he was a Conqueror over death and the grave, the Prince of Life, an impression which lay at the bottom of their future ministry. Such a resuscitation could only have weakened the impression which he had made upon them in life and in death, at the most could only have given it an elegiac voice, but could by no possibility

have changed their sorrow into enthusiasm, have elevated their reverence into worship.[5]

Strauss's critique really put the nails in the coffin for the apparent death theory. Again, I want to emphasize that no contemporary scholar would support such a theory; it has been dead over a hundred years. Only in propaganda from behind the Iron Curtain or in sensationalist books in the popular press does such a theory still find expression.

THE WRONG TOMB THEORY

The last important attempt to explain away the evidence for the resurrection was *the wrong tomb theory*. Kirsopp Lake's study *The Historical Evidence for the Resurrection of Jesus Christ* (1907) was the last work on the resurrection from the old liberal school of theology, which had grown up in the late 1800s. That school of theology sought to reduce Christianity to "the fatherhood of God and the brotherhood of man." One observer accurately characterized the theology of the old liberal school in this way: a God without wrath leads men without sin into a kingdom without judgment by means of a Christ without a cross.

Liberal theology could not survive World War I, which brought home in a terrible way the grim reality of man's sinfulness. Its downfall was largely brought about by the writings of one man, Karl Barth. As a young pastor trained in liberal theology, Barth found that he could not climb into the pulpit Sunday after Sunday to preach on the goodness of man when bombs could be heard exploding in the distance. Perhaps the turning point came on October 3, 1914, when a group of ninety-three German intellectuals signed the petition "An die Kulturwelt," endorsing the war policies of Kaiser Wilhelm II, including those that involved the murder of Belgian civilians and the destruction of the priceless collections of the library at Louvain.[6] Among the signatures on the petition were the names of the greatest liberal theologians, who had talked so much about the love of God and brotherhood of man. For Barth, that was a black day. He was later to write, "Among the signatures I found to my horror the names of nearly all my theological teachers whom up to then I had religiously honored. I perceived that . . . at least for me the theology of the 19th century had no future."[7] In Barth's commentary on Romans (1919) he boldly re-affirmed the sinfulness of man, which theological liberalism had glossed over, and he thus wrought a revolution in theology.

But back to Kirsopp Lake. As a liberal theologian, he rejected the physical resurrection in favor of the doctrine of the immortality of the soul alone.[8] Hence, he was forced to explain away the evidence for the empty tomb of Jesus in another way. He held that the women went to the wrong tomb on Sunday morning and found the caretaker in this tomb. He said something like, "You're looking for Jesus of Nazareth. He is not here." The women, however, were so rattled that they fled. Afterward the disciples saw visions of Jesus, and the women's story was twisted into the discovery of the empty tomb.

Lake's theory, however, generated little following and has been universally rejected by contemporary critics:

1. According to the gospel accounts, the women noted precisely where Jesus was laid (Luke 23:55) because they intended to return Sunday morning to visit the grave. It is therefore improbable that they would have gone to the wrong tomb.

2. Lake selects arbitrarily the facts he wants to believe. For example, he accepts the words "He is not here; behold, here is the place where they laid Him" but quietly passes over "He has risen." Moreover, the fact that Mark refers to the angel at the tomb as a "young man" does not mean he was an ordinary human figure. The Greek word here is often used of angels,[9] and the white robe in which he was dressed is the typical Jewish portrait of angels.[10] All the other gospels agree that the figure in the tomb was an angel, and the women's

reaction of fear confirms that he was. Biblical scholars agree that Mark intends the man to be an angel. There is, therefore, really no ground for believing that the women ran into the caretaker, who pointed them to the other tomb. Lake's reconstruction is clever, but arbitrarily selective and without foundation.

3. The decisive consideration against the wrong tomb theory, however, is that a later check would have revealed the error at once. Indeed, one wonders why the women did not, after their initial fright, go to the correct tomb. In any event, the disciples themselves would have checked it out later. They never could have believed in the resurrection with Jesus' body still in the tomb. And even if the disciples had not looked at the tomb, the Jews would have done that duty for them. If the resurrection was a colossal mistake based on the women's error, then the enemies of Christianity would have been more than happy to point that out, indicating where the correct tomb was or maybe even exhuming the body. The idea that the resurrection stemmed from the women's going to the wrong tomb is too shallow.

What all these alternative theories to the resurrection have in common is that they grant the substantial reliability of the gospel accounts. Granted that the disciples found the empty tomb and saw appearances of Jesus, how is that to be explained? Modern scholarship has rejected across the board these attempts to explain away the empty tomb and appearances. These theories are no longer the issue.

THE LEGEND THEORY

Since the time of D. F. Strauss, the prevailing theory in denial of the resurrection has been that *the accounts themselves are legendary*. Strauss saw that it was hopeless to grant the facts and then try to cook up some natural explanation for them. Once the skeptic granted the basic historical reliability of the gospel accounts, his case was lost. Strauss therefore denied the apostolic authorship of the gospels and rejected their accounts as unhistorical legends.[11] There never was an empty tomb, nor was there ever any guard around it. These are legendary stories that built up over the years. Similarly, the stories of Jesus' appearances in the gospels are just legends. Strauss did admit that the disciples must have seen something (otherwise the list of witnesses to the appearances of Jesus in 1 Corinthians 15: 3-8 cannot be explained), but he dismisses these as hallucinations on the part of the disciples. Strauss believed that after Jesus' death, the disciples went back to Galilee. By reading the Old Testament, they became convinced that the Messiah would die and rise from the dead. Since they believed Jesus was the Messiah, they thought he would surely rise. So eventually they had hallucinations of him. Much later they returned to Jerusalem to preach the resurrection, and by that time the location of Jesus' tomb had apparently been forgotten. The gospel accounts that we have were written much later and are unhistorical legends that accumulated over the years.

This then is the real issue in contemporary scholarship. The position of the most influential New Testament critic of this century, Rudolf Bultmann, with regard to the resurrection is virtually indistinguishable from that of Strauss. Modern critics who deny the resurrection have followed Strauss in arguing that the resurrection of Jesus is a legend.

In summary, then, we have seen that the history of the debate over the resurrection of Jesus has produced several dead ends in the attempt to explain away the evidence of the resurrection. The conspiracy theory, the apparent death theory, the wrong tomb theory, and their variations have all proved inadequate as plausible alternative explanations for the resurrection. This is of great help to us because it clears the ground for a consideration of the really crucial issue facing us today. This is Strauss's alternative: that the resurrection of Jesus is a legend. Modern critics who deny the resurrection have stuck on Strauss's position. If it fails, then the evidence for Jesus' resurrection can no longer be denied. In the next three chapters, therefore, we shall conduct a searching examination of this position through a critical sifting of the positive evidence for the resurrection.

NOTES

1. Eusebius *Demonstratio evangelica* 3. 4, 5.
2. H. S. Reimarus, *Reimarus: Fragments*, trans. R. S. Fraser, Lives of Jesus Series (London: SCM, 1971), pp. 172, 212.
3. William Paley, *A View of the Evidences of Christianity*, 5th ed., 2 vols., 1796, reprint (Westmead, England: Gregg International, 1970).
4. Quintillian *Declamationes maiores* 6. 9.
5. David Friedrich Strauss, *A New Life of Jesus*, authorized trans., 2d ed., 2 vols. (London: Williams & Norgate, 1879), 1:412.
6. *Frankfurter Zeitung*, 4 October, 1914, p. 2.
7. Karl Barth, "Evangelical Theology in the 19th Century," *Scottish Journal of Theology: Occasional Papers* 8 (1959): 58.
8. Kirsopp Lake, *The Historical Evidence for the Resurrection of Jesus Christ* (London: Williams & Norgate, 1907), pp. 247-79.
9. See 2 Maccabees 3:26, 33; Luke 24:4; Gospel of Peter 9; Josephus *Antiquities of the Jews* 5. 277.
10. See, for example, Revelation 9:13; 10:1.
11. David Friedrich Strauss, *The Life of Jesus Critically Examined*, trans. George Eliot, ed. with an Introduction by Peter C. Hodgson, Lives of Jesus Series (London: SCM Press, 1973), pp. 57-89, 565-782.

3

The Empty Tomb

The historical evidence for the resurrection of Jesus consists primarily in the evidence supporting three main facts: the empty tomb of Jesus, the appearances of Jesus to his disciples, and the origin of the Christian faith. If it can be shown that the tomb of Jesus was found empty, that He did appear to His disciples and others after His death, and that the origin of the Christian faith cannot be explained adequately apart from His historical resurrection, then if there is no plausible natural explanation for these facts, one is amply justified in concluding that Jesus really did rise from the dead.

Some modern theologians have objected to this conclusion because it *infers* from the facts that Jesus rose from the dead, and we are not bound to accept that inference. But not only would such an objection destroy all knowledge of history whatsoever, it would also destroy virtually all knowledge in practical affairs, thus making life impossible. For example, if one day we heard shots from a neighbor's house and saw a man fleeing from the house, and if we found our neighbor dead on the living room floor, and if the police apprehended the fleeing man, and fingerprint and ballistics tests showed that he was carrying the murder weapon, then, if these theologians were correct, we could still not conclude that he shot our neighbor, since this is an inference. But such evidence is accepted in any court of law. The point is that the truth of an inference should be proved beyond any *reasonable* doubt.

So with the resurrection. If we saw a friend killed and attended his funeral, and if a few days later his grave was found empty and he appeared and spoke to us on several occasions, then, as E. L. Bode remarks in his excellent study

45

on the historical evidence for the empty tomb, the inference
that he has been raised to life would not seem to be
unwarranted or merely subjective.[1] Therefore, it only
remains to be seen whether in fact the evidence for Jesus'
resurrection is of such a quality.

THE FACT OF THE EMPTY TOMB

In this chapter I want to consider with you the historical
evidence in support of the empty tomb. That evidence may
be considered under ten main headings.

1. *The historical reliability of the account of Jesus' burial
supports the empty tomb.* If it can be shown that the story of
Jesus' burial in the tomb is basically reliable, then the fact that
the tomb was later found empty is also close at hand. For if
the burial account is reliable, then the site of Jesus' grave was
well known. But in that case, the tomb must have been
empty when the disciples began to preach the resurrection,
for several reasons. In the first place, the disciples themselves could never have believed in the resurrection of Jesus
when faced with a tomb containing His corpse. In the second
place, no one would have believed them, even if they had
claimed that He was risen, since it would have been stupid
(in fact, impossible) for anyone to believe a man had been
raised from the dead when His body was still in the grave.
And in the third place, the disciples' opponents would have
exposed the whole affair as a sham by displaying the body of
Jesus, perhaps even parading it through the streets of
Jerusalem, thus bringing the Christian heresy to a sudden
and grisly end.

If the burial account is historically credible, the fact of the
empty tomb is nearly proved. Those who deny the empty
tomb, such as the German theologian Hans Grass, realize
this and thus are forced to argue at length against the burial
account as well. Unfortunately for them, however, the burial
account is widely recognized to be one of the most
historically reliable narratives concerning Jesus' suffering
and death, and their arguments have therefore something of

an air of desperation about them. The evidence for the historical reliability of the burial story may be summarized in ten statements.

a) Paul's testimony provides early evidence for the historicity of Jesus' burial. In 1 Corinthians 15:3-5 Paul quotes an early Christian saying that summarizes the content of the earliest Christian preaching:

> For I delivered to you as of first importance what I also received,
> that Christ died for our sins according to the Scriptures,
> and that He was buried,
> and that He was raised on the third day according to the Scriptures,
> and that He appeared to Cephas, then to the twelve.[2]

After quoting this saying, Paul continues the list of witnesses: "Then He appeared to more than five hundred brethren at one time, most of whom remain until now, but some have fallen asleep; then He appeared to James, then to all the apostles; and last of all, as it were to one untimely born, He appeared to me also" (1 Corinthians 15:6-8).

Paul wrote 1 Corinthians about A.D. 55, but the saying he quotes goes back even further. Since he says in 1 Corinthians 15:11 that all the apostles preach what is here summarized, it is likely that the saying stems from the earliest days of the Christian fellowship (*church* would be an inappropriate word) in Jerusalem. The apostles included Peter and the other disciples and perhaps even Jesus' own brothers (see 1 Corinthians 9:5). Thus, this saying summarizes the preaching of the original disciples themselves.

This conclusion is confirmed by comparing the disciples' sermons recorded in the book of Acts with the summary quoted by Paul: the summary is like an outline on which the sermons are built. Since the material in the sermons is quite old, the summary quoted by Paul must be very old as well.

In fact, from information supplied elsewhere by Paul, we have a good idea of just how old this saying is. Jesus was crucified about A.D. 30. In A.D. 33 Paul became a Christian when he saw an appearance of Jesus on the way to Damascus in Syria. In Galatians 1:18 Paul mentions that three years after his conversion (thus, A.D. 36) he went to Jerusalem and visited Cephas (that is, Peter) and James for two weeks. If Paul had not already received this saying from Christians in Damascus (which I think is probable, as he spent three years there), then he must have received it during this visit to Jerusalem. For Paul spent two weeks with Peter and spoke with James, both of whom claimed to have seen Jesus alive from the dead; therefore, in the words of the great Cambridge New Testament scholar C. H. Dodd, "We may presume that they did not spend all their time talking about the weather."[3] The facts about Jesus' life, death, and resurrection must have been the center of their discussion.

As a matter of fact, the very word Paul uses to describe this visit is a term used by Greek writers to designate fact-finding missions to well-known cities and sites of interest for the purpose of obtaining first-hand information about them. This suggests that Paul went to Jerusalem specifically in order to gain information about his faith from first-hand witnesses. If he had not already heard the saying in Damascus, Paul probably received it from Peter and James during this visit. It is interesting that the two individuals mentioned by Paul in his list of witnesses to the resurrection appearances (1 Corinthians 15:5-8) are Peter and James.

The upshot of all this is that the Christian saying quoted by Paul must have been in circulation prior to his visit in A.D. 36 and thus must have been formulated *within the first five years after Jesus' death.*

Now in this saying, the second line is that "he was buried." Some theologians wish to say that this does not refer to the burial of Jesus in the tomb, but merely underlines the fact of his death, as if to say, "He was dead-and-buried." The evidence, however, stands against such an interpretation. Notice the structure of the saying. It consists of four lines each beginning with "and that." The repetition of those words is grammatically unnecessary and indeed most English translations smooth out the saying by omitting them. But why did the drafters of the saying repeat that grammatically unnecessary phrase before each line? The most likely answer is that they wanted to emphasize the equal weight of each line and order them in a series. In other words, reference to the burial is not meant merely to underline the death, but stands as a separate and independent event in the chain of events concerning Jesus' death and resurrection.

This conclusion is confirmed by the chronological succession of one event after another: the events follow each other in chronological order, and the appearances are joined by "then . . . then . . . then . . . last of all" (1 Corinthians 15:5-8). Each event is distinct, and they are arranged chronologically. This makes it probable that the burial referred to here is a particular event.

These considerations suggest that the second line of this old saying refers to the burial of Jesus. But was that burial the same event as that described in the gospels? I think the decisive answer to that question comes by comparing the saying with the sermons in Acts, especially Acts 13:28-31, and with the resurrection narratives in the gospels. Notice that the order of events is identical and that the second line of the summary corresponds with the account of the burial in the tomb.

1 Cor. 15:3-5	Acts 13:28-31	Mark 15:37-16:8
Christ died	Though they found no ground for putting Him to death, they asked Pilate that He be executed.	And Jesus uttered a loud cry, and breathed His last.
He was buried	They took him down from the cross and laid Him in a tomb.	And Joseph bought a linen sheet, took Him down, wrapped Him in the linen sheet, and laid

		Him in a tomb.
He was raised	But God raised Him from the dead.	"He has risen; He is not here; behold, here is the place where they laid Him."
He appeared	And for many days He appeared to those who came up with Him from Galilee to Jerusalem, the very ones who are now His witnesses to the people.	"But go, tell His disciples and Peter, 'He is going before you into Galilee; there you will see Him.'"

This remarkable correlation shows convincingly that the burial mentioned in the summary statement quoted by Paul refers to the event that is described in the gospels as Jesus' burial in the tomb.

If such is the case, then it is virtually impossible to deny the historicity of Jesus' burial in the tomb. In the first place, given the age and origin of the Christian saying, there was simply no time for legend to arise. The saying records what was common knowledge concerning Jesus' burial, among all residents of Jerusalem at that time. Second, the women who witnessed the burial (Mark 15:47) were members of the early Christian fellowship in which the saying was drafted. Thus, if the women's observing the burial in the tomb proves to be historical, then their testimony guarantees the accuracy of the saying. (I shall examine the evidence for the women's role later.) Third, Paul's own quotation of the saying confirms its accuracy. When Paul quoted those old sayings, he knew the broader context that the sayings summarized. (Look, for example, at his detailed knowledge of Jesus' words at the Last Supper as Paul records them in 1 Corinthians 11:23-26.) That alone makes it probable that he knew the burial story

summarized by the second line of the saying. This conclusion is confirmed by his two-week visit to Jerusalem in A.D.
36, for he would certainly have learned by then what
happened to Jesus after He had been crucified. Thus, in
quoting the saying that refers to the burial of Jesus in the
tomb, Paul sets his stamp of approval on its accuracy. Hence,
the information furnished by Paul in 1 Corinthians 15:3-5
provides early and reliable evidence that Jesus was buried in
the tomb as the gospels report.

*b) The burial account was part of the source material used by
Mark in his description of Jesus' sufferings and death and is
therefore very early.* Reading through the gospels, one notices
that they seem to be made up of many somewhat disconnected, self-sufficient stories about Jesus. But the part about
Jesus' sufferings, crucifixion, death, and burial, is related in a
smooth, continuous narrative. That suggests that the narrative is all of one piece and already existed before the gospel
writers sat down to write their gospels. The story of Jesus'
sufferings and death was thus part of the source material
they used in writing their gospels. Mark's gospel is generally
held by biblical scholars to be the earliest of the four gospels.
Although its exact date is disputed, it is dated by most
scholars around A.D. 70. That means that the story of Jesus'
sufferings and death is even older than that, since it was one
of Mark's sources. Because the story describes the final days
of Jesus' life in Jerusalem, it is likely that the account goes
back to the early days of the Christian fellowship there. That
makes it a very valuable historical source, since its age and
place of origin make it improbable that legend could have yet
arisen so as to obliterate the facts.

It is now universally acknowledged that the burial account
was part of that story, which was used as source material by
Mark. There is no break at all between Mark's description of
Jesus' death (Mark 15:33-41) and his description of Jesus'
burial (Mark 15:42-47). It is a continuous narrative, and there
is no reason to think that Mark's source ended abruptly with
Jesus' death without telling of His burial. That means that the

burial account is very old and therefore probably historically reliable. The story of the burial is as reliable as the story of the crucifixion itself, since they were really part of the same story.

Moreover, since the burial account is part of the story of Jesus' sufferings and death, and since that story is quite old, we can be sure Paul knew the story. He was a contemporary of the story and was in close contact with his Christian friends and fellow-workers in the fellowship in Jerusalem. This confirms the fact that the burial referred to in the Christian saying that Paul quotes is identical to the burial of Jesus in the tomb, as described in the gospel story. The age and origin of the Christian saying on the one hand and the age and origin of the story of Jesus' sufferings and death on the other hand together insure the historical reliability of the account of Jesus' burial. And we also have the testimony of the apostle Paul to vouch for the account's accuracy.

c) The story itself is simple and lacks signs of significant legendary development. Perhaps at this point it would be helpful to give Mark's account of the burial:

> And when evening had already come because it was the preparation day, that is, the day before the Sabbath, Joseph of Arimathea came, a prominent member of the Council, a man who was himself waiting for the kingdom of God; and he gathered up courage and went in before Pilate, and asked for the body of Jesus. And Pilate wondered if He was dead by this time, and summoning the centurion, he questioned him as to whether He was already dead. And ascertaining this from the centurion, he granted the body to Joseph. And Joseph bought a linen sheet, took Him down, wrapped Him in the linen sheet, and laid Him in a tomb which had been hewn out in the rock; and he rolled a stone against the entrance of the tomb. And Mary Magdalene and Mary the mother of Joses were looking on to see where He was laid. [Mark 15:42-47]

The account is simple and straightforward and does not appear to be colored by legendary influences. Even the radical skeptic Rudolf Bultmann wrote of this narrative,

"This is an historical account which creates no impression of being a legend apart from the women who appear again as witnesses in v. 47, and vv. 44, 45 which Matthew and Luke in all probability did not have in their Mark."[4] The highly respected commentator on Mark, Vincent Taylor, says that Bultmann's judgment is "a notable understatement." Taylor asserts, "The narrative belongs to the best tradition."[5] That means that the burial account is basically a factual report of what took place.

If that were not enough, we have additional confirmation of the main points of Mark's account by comparing it with John's account (John 19:38-42). For although Luke and Matthew may have read and used Mark's account of the burial in writing their own accounts, John's account seems to be independent of the other three. John's story coincides with the main features of Mark's story: that late on the day of preparation, Joseph of Arimathea asked for and received permission from Pilate to take the body of Jesus, that he did so, wrapping the body in linen, and that he laid the body in a tomb. This historical core does not show legendary traces and seems to be a straightforward, factual report.

d) *The burial of Jesus by Joseph of Arimathea is probably historical.* Arimathea is likely to be the town Ramathaion-zophim, just north of Jersusalem. Joseph is said to be a member of the Council, that is, the Sanhedrin, which was a sort of Jewish Supreme Court that tried cases dealing with Jewish law. The Great Sanhedrin, which tried important life-and-death cases, consisted of seventy-one prominent and influential men. Even the most skeptical scholars acknowledge that Joseph was probably the genuine, historical individual who buried Jesus, since it is unlikely that early Christian believers would invent an individual, give him a name and nearby town of origin, and place that fictional character on the historical council of the Sanhedrin, whose members were well known.

In addition, some of the gospels' descriptions of Joseph receive confirmation through incidental details. For example,

Matthew says that Joseph was "a rich man" (Matthew 27:57). That fact is confirmed by the type and location of the tomb in which he buried Jesus, as we shall see in a moment. To afford the kind of tomb described in the gospels, Joseph must have been wealthy, just as Matthew says. It is also probable that Joseph was at least some sort of sympathizer of Jesus. Although both Matthew and John state that Joseph was a disciple of Jesus (Matthew 27:57; John 19:38; John adds, "a secret one, for fear of the Jews"), that description is often said to be a legendary development of Mark's more simple expression that Joseph was "waiting for the kingdom of God" (Mark 15:43). Now Mark's expression could mean that Joseph was merely a pious Jew who was waiting for the Messiah. On the other hand, the coming of the kingdom of God are the very words Mark uses to describe Jesus' gospel (Mark 1:14-15), and it is not evident that Mark thought a person could really be looking for the coming of the kingdom of God without being a believer in Jesus. Thus, his expression could mean the same thing stated more clearly by Matthew and John.

More important, however, Joseph's actions as described by Mark do seem to show that Joseph had a special care for Jesus. Mark says he went in bravely (or dared to go) to Pilate and asked for the body of Jesus. The authorities did not ordinarily give over the corpse of a victim executed for a major crime, so it took courage for Joseph to ask for Jesus' body. According to Mark, Joseph apparently gave Jesus a proper burial. There is no indication of hurry in Mark's burial account; Joseph buys a shroud, wraps the body in it, lays it in the tomb, and rolls a stone across the door. As Joseph rolls the stone over the door to the tomb, there is a sense of completeness and finality—there is no hint of a hasty or unfinished burial. Now all that is very remarkable, for the Jewish practice of burying executed criminals was simply to throw the bodies into shallow, dirt graves in a plot reserved for that purpose. Outside the city were two sites for the burial of criminals, one for those stoned or burned and one for the decapitated or hanged.[6] There the bodies could be disposed of in dirt graves. Instead of getting rid of Jesus' corpse in that way, Joseph wrapped and laid the body in a tomb, which, we shall see, was of the most expensive variety and probably his own. These are not the actions of a cold delegate of the Sanhedrin who had been assigned to dispose of the bodies.

That Joseph was giving special care to Jesus' body is also evident from the fact that he apparently did nothing to dispose of the bodies of the two thieves crucified with Jesus (Mark 15:27, 32). It seems Joseph was content to leave their burial to the Romans. But he took it upon himself to care specifically for Jesus' body. That he dared to go to Pilate and ask specifically for Jesus' body strongly suggests that Joseph did indeed have sympathies with Jesus.

Finally it is important to remember that Matthew and John state independently that Joseph was a disciple of Jesus. They did not both come upon this idea out of the blue; they had sources of information, and these sources may well be correct. John says elsewhere that many of the authorities believed in Jesus but were afraid to confess the fact openly (John 12:42-43), and he describes Joseph in the same terms. Joseph's actions as described by Mark indicate that Joseph did indeed have deep feelings for Jesus and that he was therefore at least a secret sympathizer of the man, if not a secret disciple.

e) Jesus' burial in a tomb is probably historical. Archaeological discoveries have revealed three different types of rock tombs used in Jesus' time.[7] (1) *Kōkīm* tombs, in which tunnels about six feet deep were bored into the walls of the tomb, three in each wall, into which the bodies were inserted headfirst; (2) *acrosolia* tombs, which had semicircular niches in the walls about two and one-half feet above the floor and two to three feet deep containing either a shelf or trough for the body; and (3) bench tombs, in which a bench went around the inner walls of the tomb and served as a resting place for the body. The tombs were sealed with a stone slab to keep out animals. In a very expensive tomb, a round, disc-shaped stone could be rolled down a slanted groove and across the door of the tomb. Although it would be easy to close the tomb, it would require several men to roll the stone back up the groove to open it. Only a few tombs with such disc-shaped stones have been discovered in Palestine, but they all date from Jesus' day.

When one compiles the incidental details concerning Jesus' tomb from the gospels, it becomes evident that either an *acrosolia* or bench tomb is in mind, with a roll-stone for the door.[8] This is very interesting because such tombs were scarce in Jesus' day and were reserved for persons of high rank, such as members of the Sanhedrin. Furthermore, near the church that stands at the traditional site for Jesus' grave, *acrosolia* tombs from Jesus' time have been found.

In addition, John states that the tomb was located in a garden (John 19:41). The word means plantation, or orchard, and such a site could contain rock tombs. In fact one of the gates in the North Wall of Jerusalem was called the Garden Gate, and the tombs of the Jewish high priests John Hyrcanus and Alexander Jannaeus were in that area.[9] So it could have been a prestigious burial place.

Two more details deserve to be mentioned. First, according to Matthew, Luke, and John, the tomb was new and unused (Matthew 27:60; Luke 23:53; John 19:41). This is very likely, since the body of a condemned criminal could not be placed in an occupied tomb without defiling the bodies of the family members reposing there. Therefore, Joseph would have to find an unoccupied tomb. Second, Matthew says the tomb was Joseph's own tomb (Matthew 27:60). This also is very probable, since Joseph would not be at liberty to lay the body of a criminal in just anybody's rock tomb. All the gospels give the impression that Joseph had a specific tomb in mind, and that is best explained by the fact that the tomb in which he laid Jesus was his own property.

That all these details dovetail cannot be simply coincidental. But neither can it be intentional, for the details are entirely incidental and offhand. The tomb used for Jesus' burial is consistently described as an *acrosolia* or bench tomb. Archaeology confirms that such tombs were used in Jesus' day, but only by wealthy or prominent persons. The tomb is described as having a roll-stone for a door. Again archaeology demonstrates the use of such tombs in Jesus' day, but only by the rich. John says the tomb was situated in some sort of garden, a fact shown to be consistent with the location of the tombs of notables. At the same time, the different gospel writers mention that Joseph was a prominent Jewish leader, that he was wealthy, and that he owned the tomb in which he laid Jesus. In other words, he is exactly the sort of man who would own a tomb such as that described in the gospels. The gospels also say the tomb was unused, which is plausible in light of Jewish beliefs about defilement. Joseph is said to be a secret disciple, and that makes sense of his placing Jesus' corpse in his own tomb. It is the interweaving of all those separate and incidental details that makes the historical credibility of Joseph's burial of Jesus in his tomb so impressive.

f) Jesus was probably buried late on the day of preparation. The day of preparation was Friday, the day before the Jewish Sabbath, on which preparations for the Sabbath were made. According to one Jewish peculiarity of reckoning time, a day began at sundown and ended the next day at sundown. Thus, Luke could record the time of Jesus' entombment this way: "It was the preparation day, and the Sabbath was about to begin" (Luke 23:54). That indicates that Joseph completed Jesus' burial at sundown Friday evening. According to John, that year the annual Jewish feast of Passover fell on Saturday (John 19:14). That meant that the weekly Sabbath and Passover coincided that year, so that Saturday was doubly holy (or as John says, "that Sabbath was a high day" [John 19:31]). The fact that in Mark 15:46 Joseph is still able to buy the linen shroud from the dealers shows that the Passover had not yet begun; Mark and John thus agree that Jesus was crucified and buried on the eve of the Passover.

John adds an interesting detail missing in Mark. He records that because of the impending Sabbath-Passover, the Jews asked Pilate to have the legs of those crucified broken. For the same reason Joseph placed the body of Jesus in the tomb in the garden (John 19:31, 42). Why is John so concerned about the fact that the Sabbath was about to begin? According to the Old Testament law a man executed by hanging could not be allowed to remain on the tree overnight (Deuteronomy 21:22-23) because he was accursed by God and would therefore defile the land.[10] The Jews applied that principle to crucifixion as well.[11] Thus they could not allow Jesus or the thieves to remain on the crosses overnight. So they asked the Romans to break their legs. By having the victims' legs broken, the Jews could insure that they would not remain on the crosses overnight.

That, however, created a new problem. Although Jewish law permitted burial after nightfall,[12] it did not permit burial on a Sabbath. Since the Sabbath-Passover began at sunset, the Jews had to get rid of the bodies before nightfall. It would have been most convenient to dump the bodies in the criminals' common graveyard. But Joseph chose to give Jesus a proper burial, which was possible apparently because the tomb he owned was near. Thus, according to all the gospels, Joseph finished the burial of Jesus just as evening came.

It is sometimes objected that the time was insufficient for Joseph to request the body, take it down from the cross, buy the shroud, wrap the body, and lay it in the tomb before sunset. Since Jesus died about three o'clock in the afternoon, that meant Joseph had three hours in which to work. Although there was no time to waste, it is not at all obvious that this amount of time was insufficient for the job. After all, when the gospels say Joseph took down Jesus' body and carried it away, that does not mean he himself climbed the ladder and pulled out the nails. He in fact would probably not have touched the corpse, since then he would have been defiled and could not eat the Passover (Numbers 19:11). As a man of authority, he no doubt had servants to help him. It is noteworthy that Mark 16:6 refers to a plurality of persons: "Here is the place where *they* laid him." Servants probably were the ones who actually bought the linen shroud. The burial itself need not have been very elaborate: the hands and feet had to be tied, perhaps the jaw bound, then dry spices, probably fragrant resin and powdered sandalwood to offset the stench of decay, were packed around the body, which was then wrapped in the sheet. According to John, the tomb in which the body was laid was nearby, and all the gospels agree that when Joseph finished, the Sabbath was about to begin. Hence, the pace of events of the burial is quite realistic and bears the marks of authenticity.

The fact that Jesus was buried late on the day of preparation, as all the gospels state, is therefore historically plausible in light of Jewish regulations concerning the handling of executed criminals and the burial procedures described.

g) The observation of the burial by the women is historically probable. According to the gospels, women followers of Jesus witnessed the crucifixion, burial, and empty tomb of Jesus:

Crucifixion (Mark 15:40)	Burial (Mark 15:47)	Empty Tomb (Mark 16:1)
And there were also some women looking on from afar, among whom were Mary Magdalene, and Mary the mother of James the Less and Joses, and Salome.	Mary Magdalene and Mary the mother of Joses were looking on to see where He was laid.	Mary Magdalene, and Mary the mother of James, and Salome, bought spices, that they might come and anoint Him.

It is probable that all three lists of names were part of the source material used by Mark. Mark could not have built the first list out of the other two, since then the phrase, "the Less" ("the younger") remains unexplained. The second and third lists presuppose both each other and the first list, since Mary the mother of James the younger and of Joses is identified by one son in the second list and by the other in the third list. It is unlikely that the second and third lists were built from the first, however, because then Salome's absence from the second list would remain unexplained. According to Josef Blinzler in his important study of this problem, all three lists are old and unchanged from Mark's source material.[13]

A little reflection shows how plausible this is. If the women were at the crucifixion, it is unlikely that they would not have remained to see the burial. But then the tomb must have been empty, since the grave site was known. On the other hand, if they were at the burial, they must have been at the crucifixion, since they would not show up suddenly for the entombment. And again, the knowledge of the grave site insures the empty tomb. Finally, if they were at the empty tomb, then they must have been at the burial in order to know the tomb's location. And if they were at the burial they were probably at the crucifixion. Hence, any of the three roles of the women presupposes the other two.

If this is the case, then the historical probability is that the women did witness these events, for it is difficult to see how persons who were well known in the early Christian fellowship could be named as witnesses to events that everyone knew they did not see. After all, people like Mary Magdalene and the other Mary with her two sons were real people or they were not. If they were, then how could they be falsely associated with events they never witnessed in an account that came out of the Christian fellowship of which they themselves were members? If on the other hand they were fictitious characters, then how could they have been invented as witnesses when everyone would know they never existed? The most likely solution is that we have here reliable lists of witnesses to the events in question.

Apart from all this, however, the fact that women witnessed these events is made very probable when one considers the low credibility given to women in Jewish society. Their testimony was regarded so poorly that women were not even considered qualified to serve as legal witnesses.[14] Their low rung on the Jewish social ladder is more than evident in such texts as these: "Sooner let the words of the law be burnt than delivered to women."[15] "Happy is he whose children are male, and alas for him whose children are female."[16] When one considers these facts, it becomes very remarkable that women should be named as the witnesses to the important events of Jesus' death, burial, and empty tomb. If one were going to invent witnesses to these events, then why not use the male disciples? The testimony of women was not only worthless, but actually embarrassing.

Some scholars have suggested that the male disciples fled to Galilee when Jesus was arrested and so could not be named as witnesses. But von Campenhausen and others have rightly dismissed that theory as a fiction of the critics.[17] It is ridiculous to think that the disciples, fleeing from the Garden of Gethsemane where Jesus was arrested, would return to where they were staying, grab their things, and keep on going all the way back to Galilee. According to all the gospels, the disciples remained in Jerusalem over the weekend, but lay low for fear of the Jews. When the women found the empty tomb, they were told to go inform the disciples, who were hiding out in Jerusalem. Thus, if the gospel writers wanted to invent witnesses to the crucifixion, burial, and empty tomb, they could easily have used a few of the male disciples. Instead, we have legally unqualified women playing that role. Why? The most probable answer has to be because, like it or not, they *were* the witnesses to those events, and the gospel writers honestly record the fact.

h) No other burial story exists. Hans Grass has admitted that the historicity of the burial story cannot be denied unless an earlier burial story can be discovered and the present story can be shown to contain improbabilities.[18] Grass therefore tries to point out three improbabilities: (1) There was insufficient time for the burial in the tomb, (2) the linen shroud could not have been purchased on a holiday, and (3) usually criminals are buried in a common grave. Those objections have already been answered: (1) three hours would be sufficient time for a simple burial, especially since the tomb was near, (2) Grass assumes the Passover was on Friday, but if it was on Saturday, as John clearly states, then there is no prohibition against buying goods on Friday, the day of preparation, and (3) Joseph's being a secret sympathizer of Jesus would account for his special care of Jesus' body. Grass himself seems a bit embarrassed by the weakness of his objections. He acknowledges that Mark's account is not impossible and that if it is true then the site of Jesus' tomb would have been known to both the Jews and the Christians.

But Grass claims to have discovered traces of other burial stories of Jesus. Acts 13:28-29 contains, he thinks, a remnant of a burial of Jesus by the Jews: "Though they found no ground for putting Him to death, they asked Pilate that He be executed. And when they had carried out all that was written concerning Him, they took Him down from the cross and laid Him in a tomb." This, however, is reading too much into the text: it is a remark made in a sermon and is not intended to be treated like a police report. Remember that Luke was the author of Acts, and in his gospel he had fully described Joseph of Arimathea's burial of Jesus in the tomb. Moreover, the New Testament scholar Ulrich Wilckens in his detailed study of the sermons in Acts points out that Luke has a tendency to blame the Jews for what happened to Jesus, and that comes out here.[19] In any case, this verse provides no escape for Grass because it still speaks of Jesus' burial in the tomb, so that the end result is the same: Jesus' grave site is known.

Grass also tries to read another burial story, this time by the Romans, into John 19:31: "Because it was the day of preparation, so that the bodies should not remain on the cross on the Sabbath (for that Sabbath was a high day), [the Jews] asked Pilate that their legs might be broken, and that they might be taken away." Grass is really scraping the bottom of the barrel here, for John makes it quite clear that after the soldiers broke the thieves' legs, Joseph of Arimathea came and requested Jesus' body. It is entirely possible that the Romans did bury the thieves' bodies, but John knows of no other story of Jesus' burial than the burial by Joseph.

Thus no other burial story exists. If the story of Joseph's burial of Jesus in the tomb is legendary, then it is very strange indeed that we nowhere find other conflicting stories, not even in the Jewish attacks on Christianity. That no remnant of the true story or even a conflicting false one should remain is very strange unless the gospel account *is* in fact the true story. If one denies this, then one is reduced to denying the historicity of one of the most straightforward and unadorned narratives about Jesus and giving credence to imaginary alternative stories that do not exist.

i) The graves of Jewish holy men were always carefully remembered and honored. During Jesus' day, the Jews had an extraordinary interest in preserving the tombs of Jewish martyrs, prophets, and other saints and honoring them as shrines. Therefore, it is unlikely that the burial place of Jesus would be allowed to go unnoticed and be lost. When Jesus was crucified and buried, the disciples had no idea that He would rise from the dead and leave the tomb empty. Therefore, they would probably have been concerned to learn exactly where Jesus had been entombed, so that his grave might become a holy place to them. Perhaps that is even why the women remained behind to watch the burial— so that Jesus' resting place might be remembered. Indeed, Luke writes that the women "followed after, and saw the tomb and how His body was laid. And they returned and prepared spices and perfumes" that they might go and anoint him (Luke 23:55-56). One gets the impression that the women were intent on noting the location of the tomb so that they could visit it later. Thus, given the Jewish interest in preserving the tombs of holy men, it is likely that the site of Jesus' grave would also have been remembered.

j) The Shroud of Turin confirms Jesus' burial. The Shroud of

Turin purports to be the burial shroud in which Joseph of Arimathea wrapped Jesus' corpse and laid it in his tomb. If the Shroud is genuine, then this would be dramatic evidence that the burial story is true. According to the gospels, the grave cloths of Jesus were found lying in the empty tomb on Sunday morning (Luke 24:12; John 20:4-9), and if the Shroud is genuine they were presumably kept by the disciples and handed down through the church.

One's initial reaction to the Shroud is skepticism, since the medieval Catholic church swarmed with such relics of Jesus' life, for example, nails or pieces of wood from the cross, hairs from Mary's head, bones of the saints, and so on. That makes it quite likely at face value that the Shroud is just another medieval forgery. A careful assessment of the evidence, especially concerning the tests recently concluded by a team of forty American scientists, however, render the forgery hypothesis extremely unlikely. Let us review just some of the evidence.[20]

(1) *The Shroud has marks of being authentic.* Pollen samples taken from the Shroud reveal pollen from seven types of plants that grow in Palestine, suggesting that the Shroud was once in that area. Textile analysis of the cloth also points to the Holy Land and to a very old age. The cloth is linen, normally used in Palestine for graveclothes, with traces of cotton of a Middle Eastern variety. The thread is handspun, rather than spun on a wheel, which indicates an old age. Also the thread may have been bleached before weaving, which was also an ancient practice. The weave itself is of a pattern not unknown in the ancient world, though not as common as a simpler pattern. The most recent tests, including X-ray and ultraviolet radiation experiments, have shown that the blood on the Shroud is real blood. The wounds on the body are extremely realistic. The flow of blood from the wound on the side goes around to the small of the back, appearing on the back image of the Shroud, something a forger would probably have overlooked. The angle of the blood flow from the wrist wound is also proper

for crucifixion. Ultraviolet fluorescence photographs reveal auras around the side wound and the blood on the wrists and one foot, which may be a serum which is squeezed out of clotting blood. The same photographs reveal that the body has fine diagonal scratch marks along with the scourge wounds, especially on the legs. Some observers claim that computer-enhanced photographs even reveal coins that date from the first century on the eyelids of the figure. Thus, the Shroud has many traits of authenticity.

(2) *A forger would probably not have produced such a shroud.* Although the Shroud is harmonious with the gospel accounts of Jesus' burial, a person reading John's gospel would probably have gotten a different impression. He would probably have thought Jesus' body was wrapped like a mummy. But there is no indication that this was the burial custom of the Jews, and closer analysis of John's description of Jesus' burial and comparison with John's description of Lazarus' burial (John 11:44) makes it plausible to suppose that the body was usually bound at the hands and feet, its jaw bound, and the whole wrapped in a linen cloth. But a medieval forger would probably not have known that. Nor would he have known to put the nail wound in the wrist rather than in the hand. All medieval paintings show the wounds in the hands, but this position of the nail could not support the weight of the body, as was discovered by a French surgeon in 1931. The word in the gospels for "hand" includes the wrist and forearm as well, and victims were crucified by their wrists, a fact no medieval forger could know.

(3) *There are no known means of producing the image on the Shroud.* The first photographs of the Shroud in 1898 revealed it to be a *negative* photographic image with lights and darks reversed. How could a medieval artist hundreds of years before photography have produced such a negative image? In 1973 it was discovered that the image lies only on the topmost fibrils of the threads and there is no trace of pigment. The most recent investigations confirm this, but

found that the blood stains had penetrated the cloth, indicating that the blood had absorbed into the cloth while the man's image only colors its surface. No painting could have produced such an image. That conclusion is reinforced by the evidence concerning a fire that damaged the Shroud in 1532. The heat of the fire and the water used to extinguish it would have discolored the image nearest the burn area. But there is no trace of such an effect: the color of the image is constant right up to the burn marks.

The painting hypothesis was decisively discredited as a result of perhaps the most amazing find of all concerning the Shroud. Using a VP-8 Image Analyzer, an instrument designed to study the relief of the surface of the moon and Mars, scientists discovered to their astonishment that the image contains perfectly three-dimensional data, such that the original body that produced the image can actually be molded. No painting or ordinary photograph yields such three-dimensional data. It has been suggested that the image may have been produced by a forger's scorching the cloth, perhaps laying it over a heated statue. But the problem with this hypothesis is that such a scorch would be deeper where the most contact was made, for example, the nose. But in fact this does not occur; each fibril is an identical shade, and certain areas are darker only because there are more colored fibrils there. Hence, there is just no known mechanism by which a medieval forger could have produced this image. According to one member of the team of American scientists—all of whom, by the way, were skeptical before they began their research—who was interviewed on the television program "20/20," "Very conservatively, *very* conservatively, the odds of the shroud being a forgery are about one in ten million."

If the Shroud is not a fake, then the next question is naturally: is the man on the Shroud Jesus? There seems to be little reason to doubt that it is. Why would the burial cloth of any common criminal executed by crucifixion be preserved? Moreover, the puncture wounds on the upper part of the victim's head seem to have been made by the crown of thorns that Jesus was forced to wear. Since that crown was in mockery of His claim to be King of the Jews, the presence of these wounds on the Shroud is like Jesus' signature, since no other criminal would wear such a crown. If the Shroud is not a forgery, then it is probably Jesus' image on the cloth.

How the image came to be is not important here, for I am not saying it was produced by the resurrection. I am merely pointing out that the authenticity of the Shroud would confirm the burial story of Jesus—that He was indeed wrapped in the linen cloth and laid in the tomb, which we have seen to have been Joseph's, just as the gospels say He was.

If the account of Jesus' burial is historically reliable, then the tomb of Jesus must have been known to Jew and Christian alike. And if the site of the tomb was known, then the tomb must have been found empty, otherwise belief in the resurrection would have been impossible. Therefore the historical reliability of the burial account, which is accepted by far and away the most scholars, is strong evidence for the empty tomb.

2. *Paul's testimony guarantees the fact of the empty tomb.* We saw that in 1 Corinthians 15:3-5 Paul quotes an old Christian saying:

> That Christ died for our sins according to the Scriptures,
> and that He was buried,
> and that He was raised on the third day according to the
>   Scriptures,
> and that He appeared to Cephas, then to the twelve.

We have seen that the second line of this saying refers to the burial of Jesus in the tomb. When Paul then says "He was raised," this therefore necessarily implies that the tomb was left empty.

That truth is evident from the very word used for the resurrection (*egēgertai*). Two verbs for "resurrect" are used in the New Testament: *egeirein* and *anistanai*. The main meaning of *egeirein* is "to awaken" from sleep. In the Bible, sleep is used as a euphemism for death. Thus, the picture here is of a dead person reawakening to life. The word can also mean "to draw out of," as out of a hole. Both verbs also mean "to raise upright" or "to erect." Thus, the words themselves refer to the body in the grave, which is raised up to new life. The very words imply resurrection of the body. It is the dead man in the tomb who wakes up and is raised to life. Therefore, after a resurrection, the grave would have to be empty.

Even today, if someone claimed that a man who died and was buried rose from the dead and appeared to his friends, only a theologian would think to ask, "But was his body still in the grave?" How much more is this true of Jews of Jesus' day, who were much more physical in their understanding of the resurrection! The Jews of that time believed that at the end of the world, God would raise the bones of the people from the tombs and clothe them again with flesh and give them new life. Therefore, they were very careful to preserve the bones of their dead, collecting them in jars. When the Jews looked forward to the resurrection at the end of history, they were looking forward to a physical resurrection. The idea that there can be a resurrection while the body still lies amoldering in the grave is a subtlety of modern theology. E. E. Ellis comments, "It is very unlikely that the earliest Palestinian Christians could conceive of any distinction between resurrection and physical, 'grave-emptying' resurrection. To them an *anastasis* (resurrection) without an empty grave would have been about as meaningful as a square circle."[21] Therefore, when Paul says that Jesus was buried and then was raised, he automatically assumes that an empty tomb was left behind.

That conclusion is driven home by Paul's teaching on the transformation that occurs in a person's body when he is raised from the dead. Paul taught that just as Jesus was raised from the dead, so we will also be raised from the dead "at His coming" (1 Corinthians 15:20-24). Thus, contrary to popular opinion, the Christian hope is not that our souls will live forever, but rather that our bodies will be raised up to eternal life. But in order for that to be possible, the present, mortal body must be transformed. According to Paul (1 Corinthians 15:42-44), there are four essential differences between the present body and the resurrection body:

Present Body	Resurrection Body
mortal	immortal
dishonorable	glorious
weak	powerful
dominated by the natural self	dominated by God's Spirit

Paul says that the present body will be transformed into the resurrection body: "Behold, I tell you a mystery; we shall not all sleep, but we shall all be changed, in a moment, in the twinkling of an eye, at the last trumpet; for the trumpet will sound, and the dead will be raised imperishable, and we shall be changed" (1 Corinthians 15:51-52). According to Paul, it is the present body or the remains of it that will be transformed and raised as a glorious new body. Thus, after the resurrection all the graves and cemeteries would be empty. Since what will happen to us is simply a repetition of a broader scale of what happened to Jesus, Paul undoubtedly believed that Jesus' tomb was empty. Few facts can be more certain than that Paul accepted the empty tomb of Jesus.

But now the question forces itself upon us: how could Paul have so confidently believed in the empty tomb of Jesus, if in fact the tomb were not empty? Remember, Paul was in Jerusalem six years after the crucifixion. By that time at least, the tomb must have been empty. But we can go further. During his two-week visit, Paul saw Peter and James as well as other Christians in Jerusalem. Those persons must also have believed that Jesus' tomb was empty from the start, otherwise belief in His resurrection would have been impossible, as I have explained. And even if it *were* possible, if the tomb were not empty, Paul's teaching would never have developed in the direction it did. Instead of teaching the resurrection of the body in the grave, Paul would have had to invent some theory trying to rationalize how a resurrection was possible though the body still remained in the tomb. But Paul never faced such a problem. That means the tomb of Jesus must have been empty right from the start. If the tomb was not empty, then one cannot explain how the earliest Christians could believe that it was or why Paul's teaching took the direction that it did.

Paul gives two other indications that the tomb of Jesus was found empty. First, the third line in the Christian saying when he quotes, "he was raised," probably is a summary statement of the story of the discovery of the empty tomb. We saw earlier that when we compare the Christian saying with the sermons in Acts and with the gospel accounts of the resurrection that the four statements of the saying amount to an outline of the sermons and gospel stories. What corresponds to the third line of the saying, "He was raised"? *It is the story of the discovery of the empty tomb.* The line of the saying "he was raised" mirrors the angel's words, "He has risen." That makes it very probable that the third line of the saying corresponds to the story of the empty tomb. From that fact two conclusions follow. (1) The story of the empty tomb must be reliable, for it is summarized in this early Christian saying, going back to within the first five years after the crucifixion. There was neither time for legend to arise nor opportunity, since the witnesses who knew the facts were still about. (2) Paul also knew the story of the empty tomb and thus also vouchsafed for its accuracy, since he referred unhesitatingly to it.

A second indication of Jesus' empty tomb is the phrase "on the third day." The third line of the saying runs in full: "and that he was raised on the third day in accordance with the scriptures." Since no one actually saw Jesus rise from the grave (His tomb was found empty Sunday morning, and He then appeared to His disciples), how did the early Christians know that He rose *on the third day?* Why not on the seventh day or after a month? The most obvious answer is that they found His tomb empty on the third day after His crucifixion, so naturally the resurrection came to be dated on that day.

It has been objected that the gospel stories of the discovery of the empty tomb do not speak of "the third day," but of "the first day of the week." But according to the Jewish manner of reckoning days, the first day of the week *was* the third day after the crucifixion. The Jews counted a part of a day as being a whole day. Thus, Jesus was in the tomb late Friday afternoon (one day), all day Saturday (one day), and pre-dawn Sunday (one day); hence, the tomb was found empty on the third day. In fact, when we remember that the Jewish day began at sundown, then, as crazy as it may seem to us, if Jesus had been buried at five o'clock on Friday evening, and had risen at seven o'clock on Saturday evening, the Jew could quite properly say that he was raised on the third day.

But why did the early Christian saying use "on the third day" instead of "on the first day of the week"? Here we must look into the Old Testament. In the Old Testament we find that God sometimes acted on the third day to resolve a crisis or deliver His people or perform a mighty act (Genesis 22:4; Exodus 19:11, 16; 1 Samuel 30:1-2; 2 Kings 20:5,8; Esther 5:1; Hosea 6:2). In the Greek translation of the Old Testament, the phrase "on the third day" is translated by a rather awkward expression. The Christian saying uses exactly the same awkward expression. This suggests that the saying is using the language of the Old Testament to emphasize that the resurrection was also an act of God's deliverance and might. That suggestion gains in plausibility from the phrase following "on the third day" in the saying "he was raised on the third day according to the Scriptures."

Therefore, it seems that the early Christians, having found Jesus' tomb empty on the first day of the week, dated the resurrection itself on that day. Since the first day of the week was according to Jewish reckoning also the third day after Jesus' death, then, in order to emphasize God's greatness in raising Jesus, they picked up the Old Testament expression for "the third day." Therefore, in stating that Jesus was raised on the third day, the Christian saying provides still more early evidence for the empty tomb of Jesus.

Thus, Paul's testimony guarantees the fact of the empty tomb. Paul believed in the empty tomb of Jesus, as is evident from the expression "He was raised" right after "He was buried," from the words for resurrection themselves, from the Jewish physical understanding of the resurrection, and from Paul's teaching about the transformation of the present body. But Paul could not have believed in the empty tomb if it had not in fact been found empty. If the tomb were not empty, the earliest disciples could not have believed in the resurrection nor would Paul's teaching about the physical resurrection have developed as it did. Specific indications that both Paul and the early saying refer to the empty tomb of Jesus are the correspondence between the third line of the saying and the gospel account of the empty tomb and the expression "on the third day," which refers in Old Testament language to the women's discovery of the empty tomb on the first day of the week. The fact of the empty tomb must therefore be historical, since there was no time for legend to arise, since the witnesses were on hand to prevent it from arising, and since Paul himself vouches for its accuracy.

3. *The account of the empty tomb was part of the source material used by Mark in his description of Jesus' sufferings and death and is therefore very old.* Consider Mark's account of the empty tomb:

> And when the Sabbath was over, Mary Magdalene, and Mary the mother of James, and Salome, bought spices, that they might come and anoint Him. And very early on the first day of the week, they came to the tomb when the sun had risen. And they were saying to one another, "Who will roll away the stone for us from the entrance of the tomb?" And looking up, they saw that the stone had been rolled away, although it was extremely large. And entering the tomb, they saw a young man sitting at the right, wearing a white robe; and they were amazed. And he said to them, "Do not be amazed; you are looking for Jesus the Nazarene, who has been crucified. He has risen; He is not here; behold, here is the place where they laid Him. But go, tell His

disciples and Peter, "He is going before you into Galilee; there you will see Him, just as He said to you." And they went out and fled from the tomb, for trembling and astonishment had gripped them; and they said nothing to anyone, for they were afraid. [Mark 16:1-8]

We have already seen that in describing the last days of Jesus' life, Mark employed a special source. The question is, where did this source end? With the burial? With the discovery of the empty tomb? With the various appearances of Jesus after His death? In comparing the four gospels, we find that they are in remarkable agreement concerning the events of Jesus' sufferings, death, burial, and empty tomb. But when it comes to the appearances of Jesus, the situation abruptly changes. Once again we find somewhat disconnected, self-sufficient stories like those that preceded the one long, continuous story of Jesus' sufferings and death. After giving the account of the empty tomb, some gospels narrate certain appearances, whereas others pass over them in silence. The renowned German New Testament scholar Joachim Jeremias notes that this structural difference can only be explained in reference to the events themselves: there was no continuous, smooth, running account of the appearances of Jesus because the appearances themselves were unexpected, sporadic, and to different people at different locations and occasions.[22] Instead there were independent stories by the different witnesses about the appearance(s) they had seen. Thus, the most natural answer to the question would be that Mark's source ended with the discovery of the empty tomb and that the gospel writers then added the various appearance stories.

That conclusion is confirmed by the verbal and grammatical similarities between the burial account and the account of the empty tomb.[23] These indicate that both accounts belong to the same original source.

In addition, the account of the empty tomb is bound up with the account of the burial. Joseph's laying the body in the tomb anticipates the angel's words "He is not here; behold the place where they laid Him." The mention of the roll-stone anticipates the women's question, "Who will roll away the stone for us from the entrance of the tomb?" The phrase in the empty tomb account "when the Sabbath was over" presupposes the burial account's phrase "the day before the Sabbath" as the time of Jesus' burial. In the empty tomb account, the antecedent for "Him" (Mark 16:1) is found in the burial account, namely "Jesus" (Mark 15:43). The women's visit to the tomb presupposes their being at the burial, so that they know its location. We could go on, but I think the point is clear enough: the burial account and the empty tomb account are not two separate stories, but really one continuous story.

The most convincing argument for the inclusion of the empty tomb account in the source used by Mark is that it is unthinkable that the story of Jesus as told by the early Christians could end in death and defeat with no mention of the empty tomb or resurrection. Since the resurrection was the very heartbeat of the early Christians' faith, the story of Jesus would be incomplete without victory at its end. Therefore, the empty tomb account must have been part of that story. So there are very strong grounds for holding that the empty tomb account was part of Mark's source.

We have seen that since this source was used by Mark, and Mark was the earliest gospel to be written, the source itself must be very old. Rudolf Pesch, in his massive commentary on Mark's gospel, argues that the geographical references, personal names, and so forth point to Jerusalem as the place of origin of Mark's source.[24] As to its age, Pesch contends that Paul's account of the Last Supper in 1 Corinthians 11:23-25 presupposes the account of this event in Mark's source. Since Paul's own account is quite old, the account in Mark's source must be still older and stem from the very first years of the fellowship in Jerusalem. Pesch finds confirmation of that conclusion in the fact that Mark's source never mentions the high priest by name (Mark 14:53, 54, 60, 61, 63). It is like our referring to "the President" or "the governor," meaning the man who now holds the office. According to Pesch, this means that Caiaphas was still the high priest when Mark's source was being passed around. Since Caiaphas was high priest from A.D. 18-37, this implies that the latest date for the origin of Mark's source was A.D. 37, or only seven years after Jesus' death.

If this is so, then any attempt to reduce the empty tomb account to an unhistorical legend is doomed to failure. For given the age (even if not as old as Pesch argues) and the place of origin of Mark's source, legend could not have accrued to produce a false story that people who knew better would believe. Therefore, the account must be historical.

4. *The expression "the first day of the week" instead of "on the third day" proves that the empty tomb account is extremely old.* We have seen that the early Christians began to refer to the time of Jesus' resurrection as "on the third day," probably because the Old Testament uses this phrase to describe God's mighty acts. That phrase apparently became very popular and important for the early preachers of the gospel. But here is a very curious thing: in the empty tomb story, the phrase "on the third day" is not used. Rather we find "on the first day of the week." That is extremely significant, for as E. L. Bode explains, if the empty tomb story were a legendary account that arose after a long period of time, then it would certainly have used the prominent, accepted, and old phrase "on the third day."[25] The nearly inescapable conclusion is that the account of the discovery of the empty tomb must have originated even *before* the early Christians began to use the expression "on the third day." The highly esteemed British commentator Raymond Brown observes, "The basic time indication of the finding of the tomb was fixed in Christian memory before the possible symbolism in the three-day reckoning had yet been perceived."[26] Since we have seen that the phrase "on the third day" is itself very old, being part of a Christian saying that goes back to within the first five years after Jesus' death, then the empty tomb story must be even older, incredibly near to the events it describes.

That conclusion receives further support from the fact that the phrase "on the first day of the week" is awkward Greek for a normal Aramaic expression, suggesting that the phrase is a Greek rendering of the language spoken by Jesus and the early disciples themselves. This again points to the very early origin of the account of the empty tomb's discovery.

So once again we are led to the conclusion that the empty tomb account is extremely old. Its proximity to the original events themselves make it impossible to regard the account as legendary. It is highly probable that Jesus' tomb was indeed found empty "on the first day of the week."

5. *The story itself is simple and lacks signs of significant legendary development.* Even the radical critic Bultmann admits, "Mark's presentation is extremely reserved, insofar as the resurrection and the appearance of the risen Lord are not recounted."[27] It is both amusing and instructive to compare the accounts in the apocryphal gospels written in the second century, for example, the so-called Gospel of Peter:

Now in the night in which the Lord's day dawned, when the soldiers, two by two in every watch, were keeping guard, there rang out a loud voice in heaven, and they saw the heavens opened and two men come down from there in a great brightness and draw nigh to the sepulchre. The stone which had been laid against the entrance to the sepulchre started of itself to roll and gave way to the side, and the sepulchre was opened, and both the young men entered in. When now those soldiers saw this, they awakened the centurion and the elders—for they also were there to assist at the watch. And whilst they were relating what they had seen, they saw again three men come out from the sepulchre, and two of them sustaining the other, and a cross following them, and the heads of the two reaching to heaven, but that of him who was led of them by the hand overpassing the heavens. And they heard a voice out of the heavens crying, "Thou hast preached to them that sleep," and from the cross there was heard the answer, "Yea." [Gospel of Peter 8:35-42]

In another forgery, The Ascension of Isaiah 3:16, Jesus comes out of the tomb sitting on the shoulders of the angels Michael and Gabriel. Those are true legends: they are colored by theological and other developments. The absence of such factors indicates once more that the account of the discovery of the empty tomb is a factual reporting of what occurred.

6. *The discovery of the empty tomb by women is highly probable.* Given the low status of women in Jewish society and their lack of qualification to serve as legal witnesses, it is very likely that their discovery of the empty tomb is not a later legendary development, but the truth. Otherwise men would have been used to discover the empty tomb. We have seen that all the gospels agree that the disciples remained in Jerusalem over the weekend and therefore could have been made to discover the empty tomb. The fact that women, whose witness counted for nothing, are said to have discovered the empty tomb makes it very credible historically that such was the case.

Two other considerations support that conclusion. First, the denial of Jesus by Peter shows the disciples were in Jerusalem. All the gospels record the well-known story of how Peter, after Jesus' arrest, denied his Lord three times. The story shows that the disciples did not flee from the city after Jesus' arrest. Moreover, we know from other information in the New Testament that Peter became a leader of the Christian fellowship in Jerusalem. It is unlikely that early Christians would have invented out of the blue a story of their leader's apostasy and denial of Jesus, if that had not happened. The fact that so shameful a story would be preserved in all four gospels suggests that it is true.

Second, it is equally unlikely that the early believers would have made up the story of the disciples' hiding in cowardice, while women boldly observed the crucifixion and burial and visited the tomb. The early believers would have no motive in humiliating its leaders by making them into cowards and women into heroes. Again it appears probable that the disciples' lying low for fear of the Jews was really what took place. But if that is so, then once again it is shown that the disciples were in Jerusalem over the weekend.

Those two considerations make it likely that the disciples did not flee the city, but remained in Jerusalem. A later legend would have had no difficulty in making some of them discover the empty tomb. That they do not, but instead women do, makes it highly probable that women did indeed discover the empty tomb.

And once again, the names of those women preclude the story's being a legend, since persons who would be known in the early Jerusalem fellowship could not be associated with a false account.

7. *The investigation of the empty tomb by Peter and John is historically probable.* According to both Luke and John, after the women's discovery of the empty tomb, some of the disciples investigated:

And these words appeared to them as nonsense, and they would not believe them. [But Peter arose and ran to the tomb; stooping and looking in, he saw the linen wrappings only; and he went away to his home, marveling at that which had happened] . . . "Some of those who were with us went to the tomb and found it just exactly as the women also had said." [Luke 24:11-12, 24]

And so she ran and came to Simon Peter, and to the other disciple whom Jesus loved, and said to them, "They have taken away the Lord out of the tomb, and we do not know where they have laid Him." Peter therefore went forth, and the other disciple, and they were going to the tomb. And the two were running together; and the other disciple ran ahead faster than Peter, and came to the tomb first; and stooping and looking in, he saw the linen wrappings lying there, but he did not go in. Simon Peter therefore also came, following him, and entered the tomb; and he beheld the linen wrappings lying there, and the face-cloth, which had been on His head, not lying with the linen wrappings, but rolled up in a place by itself. Then entered in therefore the other disciple also, who had first come to the tomb, and he saw, and believed.

> For as yet they did not understand the
> Scripture, that He must rise again from
> the dead. So the disciples went away
> again to their own homes. [John 20:2-10]

We have here two independent accounts of an investigation of the tomb by some disciples, which took place *after* the gospel of Mark ends. Luke names only Peter, but later mentions a plurality: "some of those." John identifies Peter's companion as the disciple whom Jesus loved. This unnamed disciple, usually called the beloved disciple, appears only in John's gospel. He reclined on Jesus' chest at the Last Supper, he was at the cross with Jesus' mother, he may have been with Peter when he denied Jesus three times, he accompanied Peter and Mary back to the tomb, and he was among seven disciples to whom Jesus appeared by the Sea of Galilee. Most intriguing, at the very close of John's gospel, this beloved disciple is disclosed to be an eyewitness to and the writer of the things recorded in the gospel: "This is the disciple who bears witness of these things, and wrote these things; and we know that his witness is true" (John 21:24). The "we" here, who vouch for the beloved disciple's accuracy, may have been a group of his pupils or colleagues. At face value the statement says that the beloved disciple is the author of the gospel and saw personally what is recorded in it. At the very least, it must mean that he is the personal source and authority behind the gospel and that his memory helps to fill out the sources of historical information that the author had. If this is true, then we are in possession of eyewitness testimony to the empty tomb of Jesus.

But what is to be made of this claim? Although some critics have asserted that the beloved disciple is just a symbolic figure, their attempts to reduce him to a mere symbol are quite comical. For no agreement can be reached by theologians as to what in the world he is supposed to symbolize. If the gospel's author wanted the beloved disciple to symbolize something, then he surely would have made the meaning of the symbol clearer; otherwise the whole thing is pointless. In any case, these critics assume that if a figure is symbolical, then he cannot also be historical, which is simply false. A historical person or event could serve as a symbol of a wider significance. Besides, the gospel's author no doubt regarded the beloved disciple as a historical person. For Peter was certainly a historical individual, and it would be very strange to have him accompanied to the tomb by a purely symbolic figure. In all the situations in which he appears, the beloved disciple is presented as an ordinary, historical person.

If then the beloved disciple is not presented as a mere symbol, but as a real person, was he in fact a historical individual? This is difficult to deny. For John 21:20-24 proves that the beloved disciple was a real historical person who was one of the original disciples of Jesus. It records:

> Peter, turning around, saw the disciple whom Jesus loved following them; the one who also had leaned back on His breast at the supper, and said, "Lord, who is the one who betrays You?" Peter therefore seeing him said to Jesus, "Lord, and what about this man?" Jesus said to him, "If I want him to remain until I come, what is that to you? You follow Me!" This saying therefore went out among the brethren that that disciple would not die; yet Jesus did not say to him that he would not die, but only, "If I want him to remain until I come, what is that to you?" [John 21:20-23]

This passage shows that the beloved disciple was well known in early Christian circles, and it was widely held that Jesus would return before this man died. So he must have been a real person, who was one of Jesus' disciples. As Brown remarks, the whole early Christian church was not holding its breath to see if a symbol or fictional character would die before Jesus returned.[28]

If this is so, then it becomes difficult to deny the historicity of the disciples' investigation of the tomb. For the beloved disciple is said to have been a witness of that event. The only way to deny this is to assert either that he lied to his pupils or colleagues about his being there or that they all conspired together to lie in writing him back into the gospel, although they knew he really was not there. Neither of those alternatives is plausible, for they collapse back into the old view that the disciples were liars and cheats, a view that simply cannot be sustained.

Who, then, was this man called the beloved disciple? Since he was present at the Last Supper, he must have been one of the inner circle of the twelve disciples. Since he was one of the witnesses of Jesus' appearance at the Sea of Galilee, he must have been one of the seven disciples present at that event: "There were together Simon Peter, and Thomas (called Didymus), and Nathanael of Cana in Galilee, and the sons of Zebedee, and two others of His disciples" (John 21:2). Since the beloved disciple is unnamed, he must have been either one of the two sons of Zebedee or one of the two anonymous disciples. We have noted already the close association of the beloved disciple with Peter. When we read the other gospels, we find that Peter and the two sons of Zebedee, James and John, form a trio that were closely bound to Jesus and to each other. That close association suggests that the beloved disciple was either James or John. But James was martyred for his faith very early on, so that he could not be the beloved disciple, who, according to rumor, was not to die before Christ's return. So the beloved disciple must have been John the son of Zebedee.

Weighty confirmation of that fact is that neither James nor John is mentioned *even once* in the gospel of John until the list of the seven disciples in the last chapter. It is inconceivable that so prominent a disciple as John, who plays an important role in the other gospels, could fail to be mentioned unless it was because he was in fact the beloved disciple. Further confirmation comes from the fact that, although other persons in the gospel of John are carefully identified, John the Baptist is referred to only as "John." That is probably because the gospel's author either knew or was John the beloved disciple and thus was in no danger of confusing him with John the Baptist. According to the respected British commentator C. K. Barrett, we may conclude with assurance that "the author of the gospel, whoever he may have been, described as the disciple whom Jesus loved, John, the son of Zebedee, and one of the Twelve."[29]

That conclusion is of tremendous significance. For think of it! That means that we have in our hands accounts of events either written by or based directly upon the testimony of a close companion of the historical Jesus and an eyewitness of such facts as His crucifixion, empty tomb, and appearances. That is evidence of the greatest historical value. For as one critic has put it, grant that even one gospel writer was an eyewitness of the events concerning the resurrection, and their truth cannot be denied. In John we have such a witness. Therefore, the fact of the disciples' investigation of the empty tomb stands on solid historical ground.

8. *It would have been impossible for the disciples to proclaim the resurrection in Jerusalem had the tomb not been empty.* It would have been impossible for a Jew to believe in a resurrection if the man's body were still in the grave. The idea that Jesus rose from the dead in a different body while His corpse remained in the tomb is a purely modern notion. As Bode emphasizes, Jewish mentality would never have accepted a division of two bodies, one in the grave and one in the new life.[30] It was the body in the grave that was raised.

Therefore, the disciples could never have preached the resurrection, nor would anyone have believed them, if Jesus' corpse were still in the tomb. And even if the disciples did not go to check out the tomb, the Jews could have been guilty of no such oversight. Even if the burial story were totally false, and Jesus were buried in the criminals' graveyard, it would not have been difficult for the Jewish authorities to locate a freshly dug grave, even after several weeks, and, if necessary, exhume the body. When therefore the disciples began to preach the resurrection in Jerusalem, and people believed them, and the Jewish authorities stood helplessly by, the tomb must have been empty. The fact that the

Christian fellowship, founded on belief in Jesus' resurrection, could arise and flourish in the face of its enemies in Jerusalem, the very city where Jesus had only recently been publicly executed and buried, is powerful evidence for the fact of the empty tomb.

9. *The earliest Jewish propaganda against the Christian believers presupposes the empty tomb*. In Matthew's gospel, we find the story of how the Jews set a guard around the tomb of Jesus and how the guards fled:

> Now while they were on their way, behold, some of the guard came into the city and reported to the chief priests all that had happened. And when they had assembled with the elders and counseled together, they gave a large sum of money to the soldiers, and said, "You are to say, 'His disciples came by night and stole Him away while we were asleep.' And if this should come to the governor's ears, we will win him over and keep you out of trouble." And they took the money and did as they had been instructed; and this story was widely spread among the Jews, and is to this day. [Matthew 28:11-15]

Now I want to draw your attention to the incidental remark made at the end by Matthew: "And this story was widely spread among the Jews." This short, parenthetical comment by Matthew reveals that he was trying to answer the allegations made against the Christian believers by the early Jewish propaganda. What were the Jews saying about the Christian proclamation that Jesus was risen? That the disciples were crazy? That Jesus still lay in the tomb? That His body was in some unknown grave? No, they said, *the disciples came and stole His body*. Think about that. His disciples came and stole His body. The Jews did not point to His tomb or even say it was unknown; rather they entangled themselves in a hopeless debate trying to explain away the empty tomb. The early Jewish propaganda against which Matthew writes thus itself presupposes and bears witness to the fact that Jesus' tomb was empty. The evidence is all the more powerful because it comes from the enemies of the

Christian "heresy" themselves. Whether Matthew's story about the guard and the bribe is historical is thus for us quite beside the point. The important thing is that Matthew unintentionally tells us by relating this story, which he felt compelled to refute, exactly what the early Jews were saying against the Christians. They were trying to explain why Jesus' body was no longer in the tomb. Thus the early Jewish propaganda provides impressive evidence that Jesus' tomb was empty.

10. *The fact that Jesus' tomb was not venerated as a shrine indicates that the tomb was empty.* I noted earlier that in Judaism the tomb of a prophet or holy man was preserved and venerated as a shrine. But it is important to understand why that was so. It was because the remains of the prophet lay in the tomb and thus imparted to the site its religious value. Of course, if the body were not there, then the grave would lose its significance as a shrine. Now when we examine the evidence of early Christianity, we find, in the words of British New Testament scholar James D. G. Dunn, "absolutely no trace" of any veneration of Jesus' burial place.[31] It was not looked upon as a shrine or remembered as a holy place. How is one to explain that peculiar fact in light of the disciples' reverence for Jesus as the Holy One of God? From all that has been said so far, the answer is clear: the fact that Jesus' tomb was empty made it devoid of any religious significance, for Jesus' body was not in the tomb. In the words of the angel, "He is not here, for He has risen!" Thus, the fact that Jesus' tomb was not venerated adds yet another piece of confirmatory evidence indicating that the tomb was empty.

Taken together, these ten considerations constitute a powerful case for the fact that Jesus' tomb was actually found empty on Sunday morning by a small group of His women followers. As a simple historical fact, that seems to be amply attested. As D. H. Van Daalen has pointed out, it is extremely difficult to object to the empty tomb on historical grounds; those who deny it do so on the basis of theological or philosophical assumptions (like the assumption that miracles are impossible).[32] But assumptions may simply have to be changed in light of historical facts. And it is interesting that more and more New Testament scholars seem to be realizing this. According to Jacob Kremer, a German scholar who has specialized in the study of the resurrection, "By far, most exegetes . . . hold firmly to the reliability of the biblical statements over the empty tomb," and he lists twenty-eight prominent scholars in support:[33] Blank, Blinzler, Bode, von Campenhausen, Delorme, Dhanis, Grundmann, Hengel, Lehmann, Léon-Dufour, Lichtenstein, Mánek, Martini, Mussner, Nauck, Rengstorff, Ruckstuhl, Schenke, Schmitt, K. Schubert, Schwank, Schweizer, Seidensticker, Strobel, Stuhlmacher, Trilling, Vögtle, Wilckens. I can think of at least sixteen more names that he neglected to mention: Benoit, Brown, Clark, Dunn, Ellis, Gundry, Hooke, Jeremias, Klappert, Ladd, Lane, Marshall, Moule, Perry, J. A. T. Robinson, and Schnackenburg. The prominent German New Testament commentator Rudolf Schnackenburg agrees that "most exegetes accept the historicity of the empty tomb, so that this question is not the decisive point in the discussion about the resurrection."[34]

EXPLAINING THE EMPTY TOMB

Since the fact of the empty tomb is well established historically, the next question can only be, How is it to be explained? Although the disciples did not at first understand why the tomb was empty (Mary thought the body had been stolen; John 20:2), we know today that most alternative explanations for the empty tomb are more unbelievable than the resurrection itself (for example, the disciples' stealing the body, Jesus' not being dead, the women's visiting the wrong tomb, and so forth). In other words, it takes more faith to believe in those theories than it does to believe that Jesus really rose from the dead.

To deny that Jesus rose from the dead as the early Christians proclaimed, it is necessary to say that some unknown party robbed the tomb prior to the women's visit. That is, of course, an appeal to ignorance, and there is no positive proof for this assertion. It also assumes that the story about the Jews' posting a guard at the tomb is not true, which would have to be proved. More important, however, there are good reasons for rejecting the theory: (1) There was no motive for stealing the body. Tomb robbers would have no reason to break into the tomb, since nothing valuable was buried with the corpse. Moreover, robbers are after the goods interred with the body, not the body itself. Why then would they carry off the dead man's body, and what would they do with it? It is conceivable that enemies of Jesus might desecrate the tomb, but again, it would be pointless for them to haul off the corpse and hide it. (2) Apparently no one other than Joseph and his companions and the women even knew where Jesus was buried. Joseph probably surprised the Jews and everyone else by placing the body in the tomb instead of dumping it in the criminals' graveyard. So no one else would know where the body was in order to steal it. (3) The time was insufficient for such a conspiracy. Since the burial was Friday evening and the women found the tomb empty at dawn on Sunday, the would-be thieves would have to hatch their plot, steal the body, and dispose of it sometime between Friday night and Sunday morning. But given the tumultuous confusion in Jerusalem during Jesus' trial and execution—and at Passover time no less—it strains credulity to believe that a group of men would get together and conceive of and execute a plot to steal the body. It sounds more like a Hollywood movie. (4) The fact that the graveclothes were found in the tomb precludes theft of the body. Remember that when the disciples investigated the tomb they found the graveclothes lying in the tomb. These clothes probably included the linen sheet, cloths used to tie the hands and feet, and a band to keep the jaw closed. The fact that these clothes were still in the tomb is proved by the testimony of John (the beloved disciple) as well as by the source used by Luke in his account of the disciples' investigation. Moreover, the presence of the graveclothes in the tomb cannot be said to be a legend aimed at proving the resurrection, since the graveclothes did not cause the disciples to believe in the resurrection: Peter "went home, wondering at what had happened" (Luke 24:12, RSV).* Only the beloved disciple believed (John 20:8), and he apparently did not tell anyone what he thought. Moreover, if the Shroud of Turin, which purports to be the sheet in which Jesus was buried, is genuine, then we have amazing confirmation of this aspect of the story of the disciples' investigation. Obviously the sheet could only have been preserved if it had been left behind in the tomb. If the Shroud is authentic, we have direct evidence that the graveclothes were found in the tomb. The fact that the graveclothes were found in the tomb would show that the tomb had not been emptied by robbery, for no would-be robber would unwrap and untie a corpse and carry off the body, naked, and limbs dangling. Therefore, the small detail about the graveclothes shows that the empty tomb cannot be explained by robbery. (5) Conspiracies of this sort almost always come to light either by disclosure or discovery or at least by rumor. Can you imagine how surprised and no doubt amused the thieves would have been when the disciples began to proclaim that Jesus had risen from the dead? It is doubtful that they could have kept their secret long. The Jews would have been more than happy for any such information. But we find no trace whatsoever of any such conspiracy, not even in the Jewish propaganda, which suggests that no such conspiracy ever existed. (6) Most important, however, the theory seeks to explain only part of the evidence. In the investigation of history, the historian always seeks the most simple, all-inclusive explanation of the facts available. But this theory only tries to account for the fact of the empty tomb; it says nothing at all about the appearances of Jesus or the origin of the Christian faith. Other additional theories will have to be developed in order to explain those phenomena. The resurrection of Jesus is a simpler, all-embracing explanation of the

*Revised Standard Version.

facts and is therefore to be preferred as the most plausible historical explanation.

In summary, we have seen that ten lines of historical evidence combine to place the weight of the evidence solidly in favor of the historical fact that Jesus' tomb was found empty on the Sunday after His crucifixion and burial. We have further seen that no natural hypothesis can furnish a plausible explanation of that fact. This alone would justify our accepting the resurrection as the simplest, most probable explanation of the fact of the empty tomb. But the case for the resurrection of Jesus does not rest on that fact alone: we have still to look at the evidence for the appearances of Jesus and the origin of the Christian faith. In the next chapter then, let us inquire what proof there is that after His death Jesus appeared alive to His disciples.

NOTES

1. Edward Lynn Bode, *The First Easter Morning*, Analecta Biblica 45 (Rome: Biblical Institute, 1970), p. 165.
2. That Paul is here quoting an early Christian saying has been proved by Joachim Jeremias, *Die Abendmahlsworte Jesu*, 4th ed. (Göttingen: Vandenhoeck & Ruprecht, 1967), pp. 95-98, and is acknowledged by all New Testament scholars.
3. C. H. Dodd, *The Apostolic Preaching and Its Developments*, 3d ed. (London: Hodder & Stoughton, 1967), p. 26.
4. Rudolf Bultmann, *The History of the Synoptic Tradition*, trans. John Marsh, 2d ed. (Oxford: Basil Blackwell), p. 274.
5. Vincent Taylor, *The Gospel According to St. Mark*, 2d ed. (London: Macmillan, 1966), p. 599.
6. Tosephta Sanhedrin 9.8-9; Mishnah Sanhedrin 6.5-7.
7. R. H. Smith, "The Tomb of Jesus," *Biblical Archaeologist* 30 (1967): 87-88.
8. Raymond Brown, *The Gospel According to John*, Anchor Bible (Garden City: Doubleday, 1970), pp. 982-83.
9. Josephus *Jewish War* 5. 147, 259.

10. See also Mishnah Sanhedrin 6.6; B. Sanhedrin 46b Bar; and Josephus *Antiquities of the Jews* 4. 202.
11. Josephus *Jewish War* 4. 317.
12. Josephus *Antiquities of the Jews* 4. 264.
13. Josef Blinzler, "Die Grablegung Jesu in historischer Sicht," in *Resurrexit*, ed. Édouard Dhanis (Rome: Editrice Libreria Vaticana, 1974), pp. 65-68.
14. Mishnah Rosh Ha-Shanah 1.8.
15. J Sot 19a.
16. B Kidd 82b.
17. Hans Freiherr von Campenhausen, *Der Ablauf der Ostereriegnisse und das leere Grab*, 3d rev. ed., Sitzungsberichte der Heidelberger Akademie der Wissenschaften (Heidelberg: Carl Winter, 1966), pp. 44-49.
18. Hans Grass, *Ostergeschehen und Osterberichte*, 4th ed. (Göttingen: Vandenhoeck & Ruprecht, 1970), p. 178.
19. Ulrich Wilckens, *Die Missionsreden der Apostelgeschichte*, 3d ed., Wissenschaftliche Monographien zum Alten und Neuen Testament 5 (Neukirchen-Vluyn: Neukirchner Verlag, 1974), p. 135.
20. See the excellent illustrated article by Kenneth Weaver, "The Mystery of the Shroud," *National Geographic* (June 1980), pp. 730-52.
21. E. Earle Ellis, ed., *The Gospel of Luke*, New Century Bible (London: Nelson, 1966), p. 273.
22. Joachim Jeremias, *New Testament Theology*, trans. John Bowden, New Testament Library (London: SCM Press, 1971), p. 301.
23. See the discussion in Rudolf Pesch, *Das Markusevangelium*, 2 vols. Herders theologischer Kommentar zum Neuen Testament (Freiburg: Herder, 1976-77), 2: 519-20.
24. Ibid., 2:21, 364-77.
25. Bode, *Easter*, p. 161.
26. Brown, *John*, p. 980.
27. Bultmann, *History*, p. 309.
28. Brown, *John*, p. xcvi; see also p. 1128.
29. C. K. Barrett, *The Gospel According to St. John*, 2d ed. (London: SPCK, 1978), p. 117; agreeing is Brown, *John*, p. 1046.
30. Bode, *Easter*, pp. 162-63.

31. James D. G. Dunn, *Jesus and the Spirit* (London: SCM, 1975), p. 120.

32. D. H. Van Daalen, *The Real Resurrection* (London: Collins, 1972), p. 41.

33. Jacob Kremer, *Die Osterevangelien—Geschichten um Geschichte* (Stuttgart: Katholisches Bibelwerk, 1977), pp. 49-50.

34. Rudolf Schnackenburg, personal letter, September 21, 1979.

4

The Appearances of Jesus

According to the New Testament, after His death Jesus appeared unmistakably alive to different groups and individuals on many and various occasions. The evidence for the appearances of Jesus may be summarized under four main headings.

THE FACT OF THE RESURRECTION APPEARANCES

1. *The testimony of Paul demonstrates that the disciples saw appearances of Jesus.* As noted in chapter 3, in 1 Corinthians 15 Paul quotes an old Christian saying and then lists witnesses to the appearances of Jesus after His resurrection:

> He appeared to Cephas, then to the twelve. After that he appeared to more than five hundred bethren at one time, most of whom remain until now, but some have fallen asleep; then he appeared to James, then to all the apostles; and last of all, as it were to one untimely born, He appeared to me also. [1 Corinthians 15:5-8].

The connective words "then . . . then . . . then . . . last of all" show that the list of appearances is chronological in order. It is interesting that Paul does not mention the appearance of Jesus to the women, which is related in the gospels (Matthew 28:9-10; John 20:11-18). That is probably because women were not qualified to be legal witnesses, and therefore their presence in the list would not only be worthless, but even counterproductive. Paul's concern is not to list all the appearances of Jesus, but the most important witnesses of the appearances. Let us briefly consider each appearance mentioned by Paul.

a) The appearance to Peter. First, he appeared to Cephas, which is Aramaic for Peter. It is very odd that this

91

appearance to the chief disciple is not related in detail in the gospel stories. Nevertheless, virtually all New Testament critics acknowledge that the event really happened. For not only is this appearance mentioned in the very old saying from the early Christian fellowship in Jerusalem, but Paul himself, who personally visited and spoke with Peter, vouches for the accuracy of the saying by quoting it. In addition, the appearance is referred to by Luke in his gospel: "They . . . found gathered together the eleven and those who were with them, saying, 'The Lord has really risen, and has appeared to Simon'"(Luke 24:33-34). According to Luke, the appearance to Peter took place after Peter had returned from the empty tomb and while he was alone. Luke apparently did not have a detailed story of this appearance, so rather than make up one (which, by the way, speaks for his honesty as a historian), he contents himself with this brief mention of the appearance to Simon Peter. Some scholars, drawing attention to the linguistic peculiarities of Luke's statement, have even argued that this, too, is an old Christian saying that may be as old as that quoted by Paul in 1 Corinthians 15:3-5.

Thus, the evidence for an appearance to Peter is good. The saying quoted by Paul refers to it, and so does Luke, whose source may be as old as Paul's. Moreover, Paul himself, who spoke with Peter in Jerusalem six years after the event, assures us that Jesus appeared to Peter. At the very least, we must say that Peter experienced *something*, which he referred to as Jesus' appearing to him. It is futile to try to dismiss this as legend. The question is, What did Peter see?

b) The appearance to the Twelve. The second appearance listed is the appearance to the Twelve. This appearance to the twelve disciples is the best supported appearance of Jesus. It is referred to here in the old Christian saying and is confirmed by Paul, who had personal contact with the twelve disciples. Furthermore, we have stories of this event in both Luke and John:

Luke 24:36-43, Phillips*

And while they were still talking about these things, Jesus himself stood among them and said, "Peace be with you all!"

But they shrank back in terror, for they thought they were seeing a ghost.

"Why are you so worried?" said Jesus, "and why do doubts arise in your minds? Look at my hands and my feet—it is really I myself! Feel me and see; ghosts have no flesh or bones as you can see that I have."

But while they still could not believe it through sheer joy and were quite bewildered, Jesus said to them, "Have you anything here to eat?"

They gave him a piece of broiled fish, which he took and ate before their eyes.

John 20:19-20, Phillips

In the evening of that first day of the week, the disciples had met together with the doors locked for fear of the Jews. Jesus came and stood right in the middle of them and said, "Peace be with you!"

Then he showed them his hands and his side, and when they saw the Lord the disciples were overjoyed.

We have here two independent accounts of the same incident; their remarkable agreement lends weight to their historical credibility. They agree that on the evening of the day on which the empty tomb was discovered, Jesus suddenly appeared in the midst of the disciples in a room in Jerusalem, greeted them, and displayed His wounds to them. The disciples were then filled with joy. Jesus' showing

*J. B. Phillips, *The New Testament in Modern English.*

the disciples the crucifixion scars is a striking feature of this appearance. The purpose was to show that the appearance was *physical* and that the same Jesus who appeared was the one who had been killed. So we have here independent claims that the appearance to the Twelve, mentioned in the Christian saying and referred to by Paul, was a physical appearance of Jesus to the disciples. That claim will merit further examination later.

c) *The appearance to the five hundred.* Here there is a break in the saying quoted by Paul, and a new sentence begins. This may indicate that the saying ended here and that Paul now begins to list additional witnesses known to him. It does not mean that these appearances are any less reliable, for Paul still received the information about them from the earliest witnesses, probably during his Jerusalem visit.

The next appearance listed by Paul is remarkable: Jesus appeared to over five hundred people at once. This appearance is not mentioned anywhere else in the New Testament, and therefore one is inclined at first to be somewhat skeptical about its occurrence. Yet the source of information for the appearance goes back to the earliest Christian fellowship in Jerusalem, and Paul, who had ample opportunity to confirm whether it occurred or not, refers confidently to the event. To make the situation even more amazing, Paul adds his own personal comment that most of these people are still alive, though some have died. This shows that he had personal knowledge of the people present at this appearance and that the appearance was not just a meaningless number on a list for him. Thus, despite first impressions, one cannot dismiss this appearance as a mere legend, for Paul personally knew of people who had been at the appearance and could give first-hand testimony about it. C. H. Dodd observes, "There can hardly be any purpose in mentioning the fact that most of the five hundred are still alive, unless Paul is saying, in effect, 'the witnesses are there to be questioned.'"[1] *Paul could never have said that if the event had not actually occurred.* Therefore, it is nearly indisputable that this appearance took place.

The event is not related in the gospels, I believe, because it took place in Galilee after the disciples had returned from Jerusalem. Galilee is a region of Israel far to the north of Jerusalem, by the Sea of Galilee, where some of the disciples had been fishermen. As one puts together the various strands of historical information in the gospels, it seems that the disciples, having seen Jesus in Jerusalem, went according to His command back to Galilee, where He again appeared to them. Although Luke does not relate any of the appearances in Galilee, he tells us that Jesus appeared to His disciples for forty days (Acts 1:3). Then the disciples returned to Jerusalem for the feast of Pentecost, where Jesus appeared to them a final time, commanding them not to leave the city until they were given God's Spirit. The appearance to the five hundred probably occurred during the period of Galilean appearances. A meeting of five hundred persons would have to be in the open air, perhaps on a hillside. It was in Galilee that thousands had flocked to hear Jesus teach, and hence a gathering of five hundred believers is not impossible. Although we are apt to picture Galilee as a rural land of sleepy, little villages, according to the contemporary Jewish historian Josephus, there were many towns in Galilee, the least of which possessed fifteen thousand inhabitants.[2] In the vicinity of such a village a meeting of five hundred people is quite conceivable. In any case, wherever the appearance took place, the evidence of Paul indicates firmly that such an event did in fact occur and that hundreds of people still living could tell what happened.

d) The appearance to James. The fourth appearance is another remarkable surprise: He appeared to James, who was, according to information elsewhere in the New Testament, Jesus' own earthly brother. Unfortunately, the gospels do not tell the story of this appearance. But Paul states that during his two-week visit to Jerusalem, he personally met James, the Lord's brother (Galatians 1:19). Thus, the information about this appearance no doubt came from James himself. There can be little doubt that James did see an appearance of Jesus.

What is really amazing about this is that none of Jesus' younger brothers, including James, believed in Jesus during His lifetime (Mark 3:21,31-35; John 7:1-10). John tells a rather ugly story of how Jesus' brothers tried to goad Him into a death trap by showing Himself publicly at the feast of Tabernacles in Jerusalem when the authorities were looking for Him. We do not hear much more about them until to our surprise they are found in the Christian fellowship in Jerusalem shortly after the resurrection (Acts 1:14)! There is no further mention of them until Acts 12:17, which records Peter's deliverance from prison. James seems to have gained a place of prominence among the believers, for Peter says, "Report these things to James." Paul also reports that when he visited Jerusalem three years after his conversion, he "did not see any other of the apostles except James, the Lord's brother" (Galatians 1:19), which seems to imply that James was also being reckoned as an apostle. Later when Paul and Barnabas returned from their missionary work among the pagans, it was James who decided how pagan converts should be treated (Acts 15:13). Paul says that fourteen years after his first visit, he went to Jerusalem to see the "pillars" of the Jerusalem fellowship: Peter, John, and James (Galatians 2:9). It is interesting that when some time later a delegation from the Jerusalem fellowship came to Antioch, where Paul was working, he referred to them as "men . . . from James" (Galatians 2:12). Finally in Acts 21:18, James appears to be the sole head of the Jerusalem fellowship and of the council of elders. We hear no more about James in the New Testament, but the Jewish historian Josephus records that the Jews illegally and brutally stoned James to death for his faith in Jesus Christ sometime around A.D. 60.[3]

Not only James, but Jesus' other brothers became believers as well. Paul mentions them in 1 Corinthians 9:5: "Do we not have the right to be accompanied by a wife, as the other apostles and the brothers of the Lord and Cephas?"

(RSV). Here Jesus' brothers are ranked with the apostles as ministers in the early Christian movement. The ancient historian Eusebius records the church tradition that the brothers of Jesus carried out missionary work in Galilee and Syria.[4] Thus, Jesus' other brothers also experienced a remarkable change in their lives.

How is that to be explained? It is historically well-founded that James and his brothers were not believers in Jesus during His lifetime. Not only do we have independent sources attesting to that fact, which is quite plausible in itself, but more important, it is highly improbable that, had Jesus' brothers been loyal believers in Him all along, the early Christian fellowship in which they served would have invented such vicious and wholly fictional stories about them in the gospels. But if it is certain that Jesus' brothers were unbelievers during His lifetime, it is equally certain that they became fervent believers after His death. How can that be? Though their brother's crucifixion might pierce their hearts, it certainly could not have caused them to worship Him as Messiah and Lord, as the early Christians did. When I think about this, I sometimes shake my head in amazement. Many of us have brothers. What would it take for you to *die* for the belief that your brother is the Lord, as James did? Even Hans Grass exclaims that one of the surest proofs of Jesus' resurrection is that His own brothers came to believe in Him.[5] This remarkable transformation cannot be explained, except by the fact that, as Paul says, "then he appeared to James."

e) The appearance to all the apostles. Finally, Paul reports, He appeared to all the apostles. It is not clear exactly what group Paul refers to here. It probably does not mean the twelve disciples, for that would be a duplication of the earlier appearance to the Twelve. According to both Luke and John, to be an apostle one must have been with Jesus from the beginning of His earthly ministry (Acts 1:21-22; John 15:27). The apostles were thus a limited group, somewhat broader than the Twelve. In time, the concept of who could be an apostle broadened to include nearly all those sent out to preach the gospel. But the appearance was probably to the limited group. Since this is the last appearance listed by Paul, it could be the same as Jesus' final appearance in Jerusalem (Luke 24:50-51; Acts 1:2, 6-11). Be this as it may, this appearance is also guaranteed historically by Paul's personal contact with the apostles.

f) The appearance to Paul. Having listed witnesses to the appearances of Jesus, Paul then adds his own name to the list as the last of all. The story of Jesus' appearance to Paul is related three times in the book of Acts (Acts 9:1-19; 22:3-16; 26:9-23). Here is the version as Luke first tells it:

> Now Saul, still breathing threats and murder against the disciples of the Lord, went to the high priest, and asked for letters from him to the synagogues at Damascus, so that if he found any belonging to the Way, both men and women, he might bring them bound to Jerusalem. And it came about that as he journeyed, he was approaching Damascus, and suddenly a light from heaven flashed around him; and he fell to the ground, and heard a voice saying to him, "Saul, Saul, why are you persecuting Me?" And he said, "Who art Thou, Lord?" And He said, "I am Jesus whom you are persecuting, but rise, and enter the city, and it shall be told you what you must do." And the men who traveled with him stood speechless, hearing the voice but seeing no one. And Saul got up from the ground, and though his eyes were open, he could see nothing; and leading him by the hand, they brought him into Damascus. And he was three days without sight, and neither ate nor drank. [Acts 9:1-9]

That is really quite a remarkable story. Paul—or Saul, as he was called in his pre-Christian days—was one of the Jewish authorities and the chief persecutor of the Christian movement. As an extremely devout rabbi, he hated the Christian heresy and the schism it threatened to bring to Judaism. He was doing all he could to stamp it out, and, according to Luke, he even persecuted *to death* men and women who believed in Jesus (Acts 22:4). Then came the amazing incident on the way to Damascus.

That the event really occurred is established beyond doubt by references to it in Paul's own letters. He tells us that he was a Pharisee, extremely zealous for Judaism and perfectly obedient to the law of Moses (Galatians 1:14; Philippians 3:5-6). As a result of this earnestness, he was involved in persecuting the Christian movement, and he carried out his task with a terrible vengeance (1 Corinthians 15:9; Galatians 1:13; Philippians 3:6). As he was near or in Damascus (Galatians 1:17), Christ appeared to him (1 Corinthians 9:1; 15:8; Galatians 1:15-16) and commissioned him to preach the gospel (Galatians 1:16; Colossians 1:25). After that event, which Paul considered his conversion (1 Corinthians 15:8; Philippians 3:7), he remained in Damascus three years before setting out as a gospel preacher in foreign lands (Galatians 1:17-21). The story in Acts mainly adds details.

Jesus' appearance to Paul changed the course of his entire life. He began to travel around the Roman Empire preaching the gospel. He gave up the prestige and comfort of being a respected rabbi and took on the life of an itinerant preacher, a life full of toil, sacrifice, pressure, and unimaginable suffering. From references in Paul's letters, we know that he was whipped five different times by the Jews, thirty-nine lashes each time (a triple-thonged whip was used to deliver twenty-six lashes to the back and thirteen to the chest). The Romans whipped him on three occasions. Once he was stoned (according to Luke he was left for dead; Acts 14:19). He was in constant danger during his travels. Three times he was shipwrecked, and once he was afloat in the water for twenty-four hours. Robbers were always a threat, as were both Jewish and pagan adversaries, who sought to kill him. He experienced great hardship, often going without sleep and sometimes without food. He was sometimes poorly dressed and had no place to stay. And of course, every day was passed under the mental pressure of Paul's intense care for the churches he founded, that they would stay true to the faith and not be led astray by false teachers and heretics. Eventually he made the ultimate sacrifice and was executed for his faith in Rome.

Without a doubt, Paul, whose letters make up much of what we call the New Testament, was one of the most remarkable men who ever lived. And it all began because outside Damascus in A.D. 33 he had an experience that absolutely shattered his former life and outlook and turned him to an unquenchable faith in Jesus. His conversion is just as remarkable as the conversion of James. And Paul tells us the reason for that change: he had seen Jesus the Lord.

All the above goes to prove that the early believers did have experiences that they called appearances of Jesus. We may try to dismiss those experiences as hallucinations if we choose, but we cannot deny that they occurred. I think we sometimes fail to appreciate exactly what we have in terms of historical evidence in Paul's letters. For think of it: here is an indisputably authentic letter from a man who knew personally Jesus' own younger brother and chief disciple as well as many other early disciples, all of whom, he says, saw Jesus alive from the dead. Why, that is astounding! We may try to explain away those experiences, but it would be futile to say they never happened.[6] Paul's list of witnesses makes it certain that on separate occasions different individuals and groups saw appearances of Jesus. This fact is virtually indisputable.

2. *The gospel accounts of the resurrection appearances are fundamentally reliable historically.* Three basic reasons support this conclusion.

a) *There was insufficient time for legend to arise.* Ever since D. F. Strauss first propounded his theory that the gospel accounts of the resurrection are mere legends, the greatest difficulty for this theory has been that the time between the events and the writing of the gospels was too short to allow legend to substantially accrue. Julius Müller's critique of Strauss has never been answered:

Most decidedly must a considerable interval of time be required for such a complete transformation of a whole history by popular tradition, when the series of legends are formed in the same territory where the heroes actually lived and wrought. Here one cannot imagine how such a series of legends could arise in an historical age, obtain universal respect, and supplant the historical recollection of the true character and connexion of their heroes' lives in the minds of the community, if eyewitnesses were still at hand, who could be questioned respecting the truth of the recorded marvels. Hence, legendary fiction, as it likes not the clear present time, but prefers the mysterious gloom of grey antiquity, is wont to seek a remoteness of age, along with that of space, and to remove its boldest and more rare and wonderful creations into a very remote and unknown land.[7]

A. N. Sherwin-White has urged the same consideration.[8] Professor Sherwin-White is an eminent historian of Roman times, the era contemporaneous with Jesus. He is not a theologian; he is a professional historian. He chides New Testament critics for not realizing what invaluable historical documents the New Testament books are, especially in comparison with the sources for Roman history with which he must work. He states that the sources for Roman and Greek history are usually biased and removed at least one or two generations or even centuries from the events they relate. Yet, he says, historians are still able to reconstruct with confidence what really happened. When Professor Sherwin-White turns to the gospels, he comments that for these stories to be legends, the rate of legendary accumulation would have to be "unbelievable"; more generations are needed.[9] The writings of the Greek historian Herodotus enable us to test the rate at which legend accumulates; the tests show that *even the span of two generations is too short to allow legendary tendencies to wipe out the hard core of historical fact.*[10] Müller challenged scholars of his day to find even one historical example where in thirty years a great series of legends, the most prominent elements of which are fictitious, have accumulated around an important historical individual and become firmly fixed in general belief.[11] His challenge has never been met. The time span necessary for significant accrual of legend concerning the events of the gospels would place us in the second century A.D., just the time in fact when the legendary apocryphal gospels were born. These are the legendary accounts sought by the critics.

This would be enough to insure the basic historical reliability of the gospel accounts, but we can go still further. Although most New Testament critics claim that the gospels were written after A.D. 70, that assertion, states Cambridge University's John A. T. Robinson, is largely the result of scholarly laziness, the tyranny of unexamined presuppositions, and almost willful blindness on the part of the critics.[12] Most critics date the writing of Mark around A.D. 70 because the Christian theology in it is quite developed and Jesus' predictions of the destruction of Jerusalem (Mark 13) show that the event was at hand. Luke must have been written after A.D. 70 because he probably used Mark's gospel as one of his sources and Jesus' "predictions" of Jerusalem's destruction look back on that event. The value of those arguments, however, hinges on certain assumptions:

(1) With regard to Mark, the first argument assumes that "the Christian theology" was not in fact Jesus' own. To say it is "developed" assumes that it was once "primitive." Actually the argument cuts both ways: one could argue that because Mark was written early, the theology is not "developed," but truly characteristic of what Jesus taught.

(2) The second argument assumes that Jesus did not have divine power to predict the future as the gospels state He did. In other words, the argument assumes in advance that Jesus was merely human. But if He really was the Son of God, as the gospels state, then He could have prophesied the future.

(3) With regard to the arguments for a post-70 date for Luke, the first assumes Mark was not written before A.D. 70. But that assumption is itself founded on mere assumptions. The whole thing is like a house of cards. At face value, it makes more sense to say Mark was written before A.D. 70,

for it seems unbelievable that Mark (whom critics agree was the John Mark mentioned in Acts) would wait thirty to forty years to write down his gospel. Is it really plausible to think that Mark would wait decades before writing his brief gospel, which would be so valuable in sharing and leaving with newly established churches as the gospel preachers went about teaching and preaching?

(4) The second argument against an early date for Luke assumes again that Jesus did not have supernatural power to foresee the future. And really, even on a purely humanistic account of the matter, there is no reason those predictions could not have been given before A.D. 70.[13] Prophets often predicted Jerusalem's destruction as a sign of God's judgment, and Jesus' predictions may have concerned its destruction at the end of the world, not A.D. 70. As a matter of fact, Jesus' prophecies are actually evidence that the gospels were written before A.D. 70, for Luke never casts the Romans in the role of enemies in his writings. In the predictions, Jerusalem is destroyed by her enemies. Since Jerusalem was destroyed by the Romans in A.D. 70, Luke must have written before that event. If he wrote afterwards, he could not have portrayed the Romans only as friends. Besides that, we have Josephus's descriptions of the sacking of Jerusalem in A.D. 70, and many of the striking peculiarities of the city's destruction are absent from the prophecies. But if the "prophecies" had been written after the event, then those peculiarities would surely have been included. So really the argument from Jesus' predictions supports a pre-70 dating of the gospels.

In any case, it is very apparent that the arguments for a post-70 date of the gospels hang together on certain unproved assumptions. If one goes, they all go. No wonder Robinson can compare the current arguments for the dating of the gospels to a line of drunks reeling arm in arm down the street.[14]

Actually several lines of solid evidence point to a date for Luke-Acts before A.D. 64.[15]

(a) There is no mention of events that happened between

A.D. 60 and 70. Luke centers much attention on the events that took place in Jerusalem, but he mentions nowhere in Acts the destruction of the city in A.D. 70. That is quite significant, considering what a catastrophe the destruction of the holy city was for both Jews and Christians at that time. A second event noticeably absent is the Roman Emperor Nero's terrible persecution of the Christians in Rome. From the Roman historian Tacitus we learn that Nero covered the Christians with tar, crucified them, and used them as torches to light up Rome at night. Others were clothed in skins of wild animals and thrown to starving dogs. It is unbelievable that Luke could gloss over that horrible persecution in silence. Still a third event not mentioned is the murder of Jesus' brother James, who was leader of the Christians in Jerusalem at the time. Since Luke records the martyrdom of Stephen and the martyrdom of James the son of Zebedee, it is unlikely that he would fail to relate the death of James, the brother of Jesus, who was much more prominent.

(b) There is no mention of the death of the apostle Paul. Paul was executed in Rome about A.D. 64, but at the end of Acts he is still alive in Rome awaiting his trial. The most plausible reason that Acts ends where it does, leaving us hanging, is that it was written before Paul finally came to trial and was executed.

(c) The subject matter of Acts deals with concerns important to Christianity before the destruction of Jerusalem. For example, one of the burning issues in Acts is the relationship between Christians who had been converted from Judaism and Christians who had been converted from paganism. The problem was whether the pagan converts should be required to submit themselves to all the Jewish laws and customs in order to be Christians. That was a great difficulty for early Christianity. After the destruction of Jerusalem in A.D. 70, it ceased to be a problem, since Jewish Christianity was all but wiped out in that disastrous event. The subject matter of the book suggests that Acts was written when that issue was still current.

(d) Acts uses expressions that faded from use early in the history of Christianity. For example, Jesus is called "the Son of Man" and "the Servant of God," titles that soon faded into obscurity. Also Christians are still referred to as "disciples" and the Jewish nation as "the people." Sunday is called "the first day of the week," another early expression. The most natural explanation for the occurrence of those expressions is that Acts was written early enough to be in touch with the climate of the early days of the Christian Way.

(e) The attitude of the Romans toward Christianity is positive in Acts. The Romans never appear as enemies in Luke-Acts; they are at best friendly or at worst indifferent. Such a portrayal of the Romans would have been possible before Nero's persecution in A.D. 64, but afterwards it would have been an obvious and cruel misrepresentation.

(f) There is no real acquaintance with Paul's letters in the book of Acts. The author of Acts does not refer to or seem to be well acquainted with Paul's many letters. Thus Acts must have been written before Paul's letters became widely circulated. That favors a date as early as possible for Acts, since the later it is dated, the harder it becomes to explain why the author does not know of Paul's letters.

These six lines of evidence combine to present a powerful case that Acts was written before A.D. 64. Since Luke wrote his gospel before he wrote Acts (Acts is a continuation of the gospel), the gospel of Luke must have been written around A.D. 57 or the very early sixties. This is a conclusion of tremendous importance, for it means the gospel of Luke was written just about the same time as Paul's first letter to the Corinthians (A.D. 55). Luke therefore ought to be regarded just as historically reliable as Paul.

"But wait a minute," someone will say. "Granted that Luke and Paul wrote about the same time, still Paul had earlier sayings and sources to go on." But so did Luke. He specifically states that his information concerning the events of the gospel was "delivered to us by those who from the beginning were eyewitnesses and ministers of the word"

(Luke 1:2). Luke therefore also had personal contact with the people who saw and heard what he reports in his gospel. Luke was probably a traveling companion of Paul's (Acts 16:10-17; 20:5—21:18; 27:1—28:16) and spent time in Jerusalem, where he could gather information firsthand from those who had been with Jesus and had witnessed the resurrection appearances. Therefore, Luke's information should be regarded as reliable as Paul's.

But more than that: since one of the sources used by Luke in writing his gospel was probably Mark's gospel, this means Mark was written even earlier than Luke. Robinson suggests a date of A.D. 45 for Mark. And of course, Mark's sources then go even further back.

When we remember that Jesus died in A.D. 30, we begin to see how hopeless the legend hypothesis is. According to Professor Sherwin-White, generations are required for legends to prevail over historical facts. But we are talking about less than fifteen to thirty years. Remember, we are not talking about deliberate lies; we are talking about legends. It is unreasonable to charge Luke or his sources with being liars.

The question is, Could legends build up around the appearances of Jesus at such a rate that by the time Luke wrote, the facts had been lost and only unhistorical, legendary fictions were left? As we have seen, the rate for such accumulation would be unbelievable and completely unparalleled in history. The development of legends requires too long for us to be able to dismiss the gospel accounts in that way. Historical experience concerning the process of legend formation thus provides the decisive answer to this question: No.

b) *The controlling presence of living eyewitnesses would prevent significant accrual of legend.* When the gospel accounts were formed, eyewitnesses to what did and did not happen were still alive. Their presence would act as a check on any legends that might begin to arise. The respected commentator on Mark, Vincent Taylor, has twitted New Testament critics for their neglect of this factor. Taylor remarks that if some critics were right, then the disciples "must all have been translated into heaven immediately after the Resurrection."[16] Those who had seen Jesus after the resurrection would soon become "marked men," who knew firsthand what had happened. Their testimony would act as a safeguard against unhistorical legends. In the same way, if persons like Mary Magdalene and the women did not see Jesus, as the gospels say they did, then it is very difficult indeed to explain how those stories could arise that they did, since Mary and the others were right there in the Christian fellowship in Jerusalem where the legends supposedly originated.

Legends do not arise significantly until the generation of eyewitnesses dies off. Hence, legends are given no ground for growth as long as witnesses are alive who remember the facts. In the case of the resurrection narratives, the continued presence of the twelve disciples, the women, and the others who saw Jesus alive from the dead would prevent legend from significantly accruing.

c) The authoritative control of the apostles would have kept legendary tendencies in check. The apostles who had been with Jesus were, so to speak, the guardians of the information of His life and teachings. It is simply unbelievable that fictitious stories of Jesus' appearances to them could arise and flourish so long as they were living and active, much less that wholly false stories could replace the true. Walther Künneth states:

> It is extremely difficult to see how the Gospel accounts of the resurrection could arise in opposition to the original apostolic preaching and that of Paul. . . . The authority of the apostolic eye-witnesses was extraordinarily strong. It would be inconceivable how there should have arisen in opposition to the authoritative witness of the original apostles a harmonious tradition telling of an event that has no basis in the message of the eye-witnesses.[17]

Invention of stories by Christians, says Künneth, would have been "sharply contradicted by the apostles or their pupils."[18] Discrepancies might exist in secondary details, the gospel writers might select or emphasize different aspects of the stories, but the basic stories themselves could not be legendary so long as the authoritative control of the apostles was being exercised. Once again, it is instructive to observe that the legendary apocryphal gospels did not arise until all the apostles had died, and even then they were universally rejected by the early church.

These three factors—the insufficient time, the controlling presence of living eyewitnesses, and the authoritative control of the apostles—preclude the significant rise and accumulation of legend, and thus go to establish the fundamental, historical reliability of the gospel accounts of the resurrection.

3. *The resurrection appearances were physical, bodily appearances.* Most New Testament critics are prepared to admit that the disciples did see appearances of Jesus, but many assert that those appearances were visions, not physical appearances. I now wish to examine the evidence specifically for the physical, bodily nature of the appearances.

a) Paul implies that the appearances were physical. Critics who wish to reduce the resurrection appearances to mere visions usually try to drive a wedge between Paul and the gospels. They admit that the appearances in the gospel stories are plainly physical, but they assert that Paul thought the appearances were only visionary. Because those critics inevitably date the gospels after A.D. 70, they say Paul is more reliable, since his letters are earlier.

We have already established that the crucial assumption of that reasoning, namely, that the gospels were written after A.D. 70, is wrong. Since a chain is only as strong as its weakest link, the argument fails. But let us be gracious and overlook that for now. What is the evidence that Paul thought Jesus' appearances were visionary? The critics usually give two arguments: the appearance to Paul was visionary, so the others must have been so as well; and Paul did not believe that Jesus rose from the dead with a physical body, but with a spiritual body. Let us examine each argument in greater detail.

(1) It is certainly true that as Luke describes it, the appearance to Paul had visionary elements. For Jesus appeared as a light and voice from heaven, not as a man walking along the road. But we must be very careful not to reduce Paul's experience to *just* a vision. For what is a vision? A vision is a projection of the mind of the beholder; there is nothing "out there" in the real world that corresponds to what he "sees." A person may be caused to see a vision by either internal or external causes, but in either case what he sees is, so to speak, "all in his mind" and has no counterpart in reality. But it is clear that Paul's experience was not just a vision. For as Luke describes it, the appearance was certainly "out there," not all in Paul's mind. Paul's traveling companions also experienced the light and the voice, though for them these were not the means of an encounter with Jesus, as they were for Paul. It is interesting to compare Stephen's vision of Christ (Acts 7:54-58) with Jesus' appearance to Paul. Stephen saw a vision of Christ at the right hand of God, but no one around him saw anything. That was a true vision. But on the Damascus road the light and the voice were really "out there" in the real world, and Paul's fellow travelers experienced them, too. If Luke's information about Paul's experience lacked the objective elements, then we would have had a story similar to that of Stephen's vision.

But in any case, even if Paul's experience were visionary, what ground is there for asserting that all the other appearances were just like it? Here the critics do not have a leg to stand on. All they can say is that Paul adds his experience to the list of appearances in 1 Corinthians 15, so they must have all been alike. But this reasoning is very weak. In adding himself to the list, Paul is not, so to speak, trying to bring the other appearances down to the level of his own; rather he is trying to raise the appearance to him up to the level of objectivity and reality of the others. Paul's experience occurred about three years after the other appearances, and we know from Paul's letters that some people were suspicious about whether Paul was a true apostle. Therefore, in adding himself to the list, Paul is saying, "Look, my experience was just as much a real appearance of Jesus as those of the other apostles." Thus, in no way does he imply that all the appearances were visions.

According to Luke, the appearance to Paul was in fact different from the others because Paul's was a post-ascension encounter. That is to say, after appearing to His disciples and others for some forty days, Jesus physically left this universe or dimension. He will come again at the end of history. Meanwhile, the Holy Spirit acts in His place. Therefore, the appearance to Paul could not have been physical like the others; it had to be in some sense visionary. But it was not merely visionary, for it had real manifestations in the world "out there," namely, the light and the voice. Paul in his letters gives us no reason to doubt that this is a fair account of the matter. Paul also thought the appearance to him was unusual, and he was concerned to raise it up to the objectivity of the others.

(2) Many theologians have thoroughly misunderstood Paul's teaching on the spiritual resurrection body (1 Corinthians 15:35-57). According to Paul, there are four essential differences between the present body and the future resurrection body:

Present Body	Resurrection Body
mortal	immortal
dishonorable	glorious
weak	powerful
physical	spiritual

The last contrast, physical/spiritual, makes it appear that whereas the present body is physical and tangible, the resurrection body will be immaterial and intangible. This, however, is a misunderstanding of the words used by Paul. The word translated "physical" literally means "soul-ish." Now obviously, in saying the present body is soul-ish, Paul does not mean our bodies are made of soul. What then does he mean? Well, elsewhere in the New Testament, the word *soul-ish* always has a negative ring to it and means "pertaining to human nature in contrast to God." It does not mean physical; rather it means natural, or belonging to human nature and self.

In a similar way, when Paul says the resurrection body will be spiritual, he does not mean a body made out of spirit. That would really be a contradiction in terms, for a spirit is precisely the absence of body. Rather, biblical commentators agree that Paul means "pertaining to God's Spirit." It does not mean spiritual in the sense of "nonphysical"; rather it means spiritual in the sense that we say, "Paul was a spiritual man," or "The Bible is a spiritual book." Being spiritual in this sense in no way implies being nonphysical or intangible.

That this is so is quite clear from Paul's use of these same terms in 1 Corinthians 2:14-15 (RSV): "The natural [soul-ish] man does not receive the gifts of the Spirit of God; for they are folly to him, and he is not able to understand them, because they are spiritually discerned. The spiritual man judges all things, but is himself to be judged by no one." Now obviously by "natural man" Paul does not mean "physical man," nor by "spiritual man" does he mean "immaterial, intangible man." The spiritual man is every bit as material and tangible as the natural man. The difference is not in their physical substance, but in their life-orientation. The natural man is dominated and directed by the sinful human self, whereas the spiritual man is directed and empowered by God's Spirit.

Similarly, the resurrection body does not differ from the present body in that it is immaterial and intangible, but in that it is completely freed from the effects of sin (such as disease, death, and decay) and is fully in tune with the direction and power of God's Spirit. Thus, the translation of the word in question as "spiritual" is bound to create more misunderstandings than it is worth. Since the word is used as the opposite of "natural body," I would agree with the

French commentator Jean Héring and translate it "super-natural body."[19] The legitimacy of this translation is shown by the fact that the *Revised Standard Version* translators so render this word in 1 Corinthians 10:3-4 in describing the miraculous manna and water that God supplied the Israelites in the Sinai desert: they "all ate the same supernatural food and all drank the same supernatural drink." Obviously, the word once again does not mean "immaterial, intangible bread and water." So I think "supernatural body" is less apt to create misunderstanding and better conveys Paul's thought than "spiritual body," which sounds like a contradiction in terms.

Most scholars who have studied Paul's teaching on the resurrection body agree that he is not talking about a body made of spirit. But many theologians persist in talking this way. There seems to be a great gap here between biblical studies and theology.

In any case, everyone agrees that Paul did not teach immortality of the soul alone, but the resurrection of the body. I challenge any theologian to explain the difference between an immaterial, intangible, "spiritual" body and the immortality of the soul. To say Paul did not teach the latter but did teach the former is theological double-talk.

Therefore, the arguments used by critics to drive a wedge between Paul and the gospels have not only failed, but actually have led to the opposite conclusion. We see that Paul did believe in a physical resurrection body and that he did not regard the other appearances as being necessarily the same type of experience as his own on the Damascus road.

But we can go further. There is positive evidence that Paul also regarded the *appearances* of Jesus as actual physical appearances.

(a) Paul (and indeed all of the New Testament) makes a sharp distinction between an appearance of Jesus and a vision of Jesus. The appearances of Jesus were confined to a brief period at the beginning of the Christian Way; they soon ceased and were never repeated. Visions, however, continued and were repeated. Paul himself had visions (2

Corinthians 12:1-7), but what he saw on the Damascus road was no mere vision. That is very interesting, for it shows that the appearances seen by the disciples were essentially different from visions, with which they were familiar.

Visions, even ones caused by God, were exclusively in the mind of the beholder, whereas an appearance involved the actual appearance of something "out there" in the real world. That conclusion seems to me to be nearly inescapable. The resistance of many modern critics to it is mainly due to a bias against the physical resurrection. But if one rejects that conclusion, then how can we explain the difference between an appearance and a vision as drawn by the early church? Grass answers that only in an appearance was the glorified Christ seen.[20] But that is patently false, for there were visions of the glorified Christ, too, in the early Christian fellowship (Acts 7:55-56; 2 Corinthians 12:1; Revelation 1:10-11). I challenge any critic to explain how early believers distinguished between a vision and an appearance, if it was not that a vision was purely mental whereas an appearance was physical.

If this is so, then in listing the appearances of Christ, Paul is stating implicitly that these were not visions, but actually occurred in the real world. This was true even of the appearance to Paul, which was semivisionary in character. Thus, Paul can include it in the list with good conscience. Paul held then that the appearances were not visions, but occurred in the physical realm.

But we can go further. Given Paul's doctrine of the resurrection body, it is probable that he thought of the other appearances as bodily appearances. For Paul held that our resurrection bodies would be patterned after that of Jesus. Since Paul believed in a physical resurrection body, it follows that when he states that Jesus was raised and appeared, he probably means *appeared* bodily, just as He was raised bodily. He could make no mistake about that, since he had spoken with Peter and James about what they did see.

Therefore, Paul's testimony certainly implies, even if it

does not conclusively prove, that the appearances of Jesus which he listed were bodily appearances. We may say certainly that they were not visions, but actually occurred in the real world. If the stories in the gospels are reliable (as we have seen that they are), then we may be confident that Paul also held that these were bodily appearances.

(b) A second indication that Paul held to physical resurrection appearances of Jesus may be seen by looking at the reverse side of the coin. Suppose there were originally no physical appearances, but only visions. In that case, it becomes very difficult to explain how Paul's teaching on the resurrection could have developed as it did. He could not have taught that we shall have physical resurrection bodies patterned after Jesus' body, for Jesus apparently had no body. Indeed, as we shall see below, it is doubtful that Paul would have used the idea of "resurrection" at all to explain such events. Mere visions of Jesus after His death, in other words, are not sufficient to explain the direction and development of Paul's teaching on the resurrection body. That confirms what we have already seen—that the original resurrection appearances were probably both physical and bodily.

b) *The gospels prove that the appearances were physical and bodily.* The gospels testify unanimously that Jesus appeared physically and bodily to the disciples. Critics who object to the physical resurrection usually say that the physicalism of the gospels was invented to counteract Docetism. Docetism was a heresy that held that matter is evil, and that therefore God could not really have become incarnate in Jesus. Docetists held that either Jesus' body only appeared to be physical, but really was not, or else that God's Spirit took control of the man Jesus, but left Him at the cross. Against the Docetists John wrote, "For many deceivers have gone out into the world, those who do not acknowledge Jesus Christ as coming in the flesh. This is the deceiver and the antichrist" (2 John 7; compare 1 John 4:1-3). Some critics say that the physical nature of the resurrection appearances was invented to counteract Docetism by emphasizing that Jesus rose physically.

That objection, however, cannot be sustained:

(1) Docetism was the reaction to the physicalism of the gospels, not the other way around. We have seen that for a Jew, "resurrection" meant physical, bodily resurrection of the dead man from the tomb. A "spiritual" resurrection would have been nonsense. Therefore, when the early believers said Jesus was raised from the dead, they meant "physically." Docetism was the later reaction of philosophical speculation to the original physicalism of the Christian believers. Ellis points out that the gospels did not materialize the appearances; rather the heretics dematerialized them.[21] Thus, the critics have gotten the true situation backwards.

(2) Docetism denied the physical incarnation, not the physical resurrection. Docetists denied that God ever became flesh; it was not the physical resurrection to which they objected. In fact, some Docetists held that the divine Spirit deserted the human Jesus on the cross and that the human Jesus then died and was raised physically.[22] Thus, it would be pointless for the gospels to invent physical appearances of Jesus to counteract Docetism, since Docetists did not deny the physical resurrection.

(3) The gospels' sources existed before the rise of Docetism. All the gospels' sources of information concerning Jesus' appearances tell of physical appearances. But Docetism arose much later and is probably referred to in the letters of John, which most scholars date A.D. 90-100. Hence, the physicalism could not be a response to Docetism, which was a later theological development.

(4) The appearance stories themselves do not have the rigorousness of a defense against Docetism. The physicalism of the gospel appearance stories is not a point trying to be scored; rather it is just naturally assumed and is found in the incidental details of the stories: Jesus' breaking bread, the women's holding his feet in worship, His coming to the disciples on the hilltop. Even in Luke's and John's accounts of

Jesus' showing His wounds, it is not said that the disciples actually touched Jesus. As Schnackenburg has said, if this were a defense against Docetism, then more would have been done than Jesus' merely *showing* His wounds.[23] The physicalism of the appearances was taken for granted, and no defense against Docetism is here in view.

(5) If visionary "appearances" had been original, then physical appearances would never have developed. For, in the first place, Docetism would not be a threat. Christians and Docetists might argue over whether Jesus was physical during His life, but both could agree that He did not appear physically after His death. Thus, Docetism would not bring forth the counterreaction of physical appearances, if the appearances were originally visionary. In the second place, physical appearances would have been offensive to potential converts in both Judaism and paganism. Jews would tend to reject Jesus' physical resurrection appearances because they held only to a physical resurrection at the end of history. Pagans would tend to reject a physical resurrection because they held to the immortality of the soul alone. Thus, had the appearances been originally visionary, the Christians would never have invented physical appearances, but would have held onto the original visionary experiences.

The considerations demonstrate that the physicalism of the gospel appearance stories is not a conscious defense against Docetism, but rather just a natural part of the stories. But we can go further than this, for there are positive reasons to accept the historical reliability of the gospel stories of Jesus' physical, bodily appearances.

(1) Every resurrection appearance narrated in the gospels is a physical, bodily appearance. The unanimity of the gospels on that score is very impressive when one remembers that the appearance stories were originally more or less separate, independent stories, which the different gospel writers collected and arranged in order. All their separate sources of information agree that Jesus appeared physically and bodily to the disciples and other witnesses. There is no

trace of nonphysical appearances in the sources, a remarkable fact if all the appearances were really visionary, as some
critics would have us believe. That strongly suggests that the
appearances were not in fact visions, but actual, bodily
appearances. The fact that all the separate gospel stories
agree on that point, and that no trace of visionary
"appearances" is to be found, weighs strongly in favor of the
gospels' historical credibility in this matter.

(2) The really decisive consideration in favor of the
physical, bodily appearances of Jesus as narrated in the
gospels is that, as we have seen, the gospel accounts are
fundamentally reliable historically. We have seen that the
time was too short for legends of Jesus' physical appearances
to accumulate, that the presence of the living eyewitnesses to
the appearances would have served as a control against false
accounts of what happened, and that the authoritative
control of the apostles would have served to preserve the
accurate accounts. If the appearances were originally only
visions, then those three factors would have prevented them
from being perverted to physical appearances. It is inexplica-
ble how a series of mere visions could be so thoroughly
materialized and corrupted into the unanimous physicalism
of the gospel appearance stories in so short a time, in the
presence of the very witnesses to those appearances
themselves, and under the eyes of the apostles responsible
for preventing such corruption. This shows decisively that
the appearances of Jesus were physical, bodily appearances,
as the gospels report.

Thus, the gospels demonstrate that the appearances of
Jesus were physical, bodily appearances. At the same time,
however, it should be emphasized that Jesus' resurrection
body possessed superhuman capabilities, according to the
gospel accounts, such as the ability to appear and disappear
at will, without regard to spatial distances. It was as though
He could, so to speak, step out of this dimension into
another, then back into this one at any place He wished.
Paul's description of the resurrection body as immortal,

glorious, powerful, and supernatural well describes the resurrection body of Jesus as portrayed in the gospels.

Both Paul and the gospels, then, combine to provide solid evidence for the physical, bodily resurrection of Jesus. Paul and the entire New Testament make a clear distinction between an appearance and a vision of Jesus. This distinction is understandable only if appearances were physical events. Taken together with his teaching on the resurrection body, this strongly suggests that Paul took the appearances of Jesus to be physical and bodily. Confirmation of that comes from the fact that if the original appearances had been visionary, the development of Paul's teaching on the resurrection body is very difficult to explain. For their part, the gospels provide unanimous, independent testimony for physical appearances and show no trace of visionary "appearances." The evidence for the fundamental historical reliability of the gospel accounts proves that the physicalism of the accounts is historically well-founded. Thus, amazing as it may seem, the evidence solidly supports the fact that Jesus physically and bodily rose from the dead and appeared to His disciples.

4. *Specific considerations make individual gospel appearance stories historically probable.*

a) The appearance to the women is historical. That women and not men should be the first to see Jesus risen lends credibility to this account. It would be pointless for early believers to manufacture a story of an appearance to legally unqualified women. In fact they are probably not mentioned in Paul's list because of that very fact. So why have such a story at all? Any conceivable purpose for this appearance story would have been much better served by having Jesus appear to Peter at the tomb. Hence, the story is probably reliable. Confirmation of that comes from the fact that fictions could not be invented about persons who would be well-known in the Christian fellowship in Jerusalem.

b) The appearance to Peter is historical. Since this appearance is mentioned by Paul, who spoke with Peter, as well as by

Luke, it is historically certain. It probably occurred in Jerusalem after Peter's visit to the empty tomb and before the appearance to the Twelve.

c) The appearance to the Twelve is historical. Also referred to by Paul, this appearance also certainly took place. Since the disciple whom Jesus loved was present, John's account must be accurate. The appearance took place Sunday evening in Jerusalem.

d) The appearance by the Lake of Galilee is historical. Since the disciple whom Jesus loved was also present there, this appearance must also be historical. It shows clearly that after Jesus appeared to the disciples in Jerusalem, they returned to Galilee, where they saw Him again.

e) The appearance in Galilee mentioned by Mark is historical. Since this appearance was probably part of Mark's source material, it is a very old and therefore no doubt reliable piece of information. It also shows that Jesus appeared to the disciples in Galilee.

The individual considerations go to confirm the point that has been demonstrated repeatedly: that Jesus appeared alive on various occasions to various persons after His death.

EXPLAINING THE RESURRECTION APPEARANCES

As a historical fact, that Jesus appeared alive after His death is firmly established. But how is that remarkable fact to be explained if not by the resurrection? Usually those who deny the resurrection state that the disciples experienced hallucinations of Jesus after His death and that those hallucinations caused them to mistakenly believe that He had risen from the dead. But such a hypothesis is quite inadequate:

1. *The hypothesis shatters on points 2, 3, and 4, just discussed.* The hypothesis cannot explain how in so short a time hallucinatory experiences could be completely transformed into the gospel appearance stories; nor why the eyewitnesses to those experiences should have had absolutely no control on the development of the accounts of what had really happened; nor why the apostles should have quietly allowed

such extravagant fictions to arise and replace the true stories. The theory cannot account for the early believers' distinguishing precisely between a mere vision and an actual appearance of Jesus; nor can it explain why or how the physicalism of the gospels could have evolved out of hallucinations; nor why the gospels should unanimously agree on this fact with no trace of the original, true experiences. Finally, the theory is broken by the evidence for the historicity of particular appearances, such as to the Twelve, which were clearly not hallucinations. All the considerations together combine to bury the hallucination hypothesis.

2. *The number and various circumstances of the appearances make hallucinations an improbable explanation.* From Paul's list of witnesses alone, we know that different individuals and groups on different occasions and no doubt in different places saw appearances of Jesus. But it is unlikely that hallucinations could be experienced by so many various people under so many varied circumstances. The suggestion that there was a chain reaction of hallucinations among believers in Jesus does not alleviate the difficulty because neither James nor Paul stood in the chain. It has been suggested that Paul had a hallucination because of an inner, personal, religious struggle. But there is no evidence of such a struggle, at least with Christianity, for Paul hated the Christian heresy as a threat to Judaism. And any inner struggle he may have had in Judaism in terms of guilt under the law of Moses (although Paul himself says confidently that he was blameless under the law), cannot explain why he would turn to the Christian heresy to alleviate that guilt. The fact is that the hypothesis of hallucinations cannot account for the variety and number of Jesus' appearances.

3. *The disciples were not psychologically disposed to produce hallucinations.* Visions require either a special state of mind or artificial stimulus through medicines in order to occur. But the disciples after Jesus' crucifixion were utterly crushed and in no frame of mind to hallucinate. In no way did they expect

Jesus to come back to life. As far as they were concerned, the last act of the tragedy had been played, and the show was over. The great weakness of the hallucination hypothesis is that it does not take seriously either Jesus' death nor the crisis it caused for the disciples.

4. *Hallucinations would never have led to the conclusion that Jesus had been raised from the dead.* We shall develop this point in the next chapter. For now I shall simply note that in a hallucination, a person experiences nothing new. That is because the hallucination is a projection of his own mind. Hence, hallucinations cannot exceed the content of a person's mind. But as we shall see, the resurrection of Jesus involved ideas utterly foreign to the disciples' minds. They could not of their own, therefore, have projected hallucinations of Jesus alive from the dead.

5. *The hallucination hypothesis fails to account for the full scope of the evidence.* The hallucination hypothesis seeks to account only for part of the evidence, namely, the appearances. But it does nothing to account for the empty tomb. In order to explain the empty tomb, one must come up with another theory and join it with the hallucination hypothesis. One of the greatest weaknesses of alternative explanations to the resurrection is their incompleteness: they fail to provide a comprehensive, overarching explanation of all the data. By contrast, the resurrection furnishes one, simple, comprehensive explanation of all the facts without distorting them. Therefore, it is the better explanation.

A second alternative to the resurrection as an explanation for the appearances of Jesus is that they were parapsychological phenomena. Michael Perry, an archdeacon of the Church of England, maintains that the appearances of Jesus could have been veridical visions of the dead.[24] What is a veridical vision? It is a hallucination produced by a person's mind when he receives a message by telepathy. Such visions are experienced by persons who have seen an individual, when really that individual was dead or dying miles away. Usually only loved ones or close friends experience such visions.

Unlike ordinary hallucinations, these visions require no special emotional mood on the part of the persons receiving them. Michael Perry's theory is that Jesus died and rose in a "spiritual body." But He sent a telepathic message to His disciples that caused them to project hallucinations of Jesus physically raised from the dead. In that way the idea of Jesus' physical resurrection arose.

The most unconvincing aspects of Perry's theory are the religious or supernatural ones. For example, we have seen that his understanding of Paul's term "spiritual body" as an intangible, immaterial substance is completely mistaken. And in order to explain the empty tomb, Perry is reduced to the hypothesis that God annihilated Jesus' body, a completely pointless exercise since Perry thinks the new "spiritual body" is entirely unrelated to and distinct from the body in the tomb. Perhaps worst of all, Perry makes God and Jesus responsible for the disastrous error on the part of Christianity in believing Jesus rose from the dead physically. One can only shudder when Perry pronounces: God deceived the disciples so that from evil, good might come.[25] As a religious explanation the theory is very unconvincing.

It would be better to take the hypothesis as a purely natural alternative to the resurrection: the disciples saw veridical visions of the dead Jesus—extraordinary, but not unique or supernatural. They mistakenly believed that He had risen from the dead. But as a purely natural explanation the theory cannot succeed:

1. *There is no comparable case to Jesus' resurrection appearances.* As Perry admits, in order to find parallels to the resurrection appearances, one must ransack the casebooks of parapsychology and build up a composite picture of striking aspects from many different cases. The fact is, no single case is fully analogous to a resurrection appearance, and even the similarities are not identical.

2. *The number of occasions on which Jesus was seen over so long a time is unparalleled in the casebooks.* Usually veridical visions occur once, at a person's death, to a loved one far away. But

Jesus' appearances were many and occurred over a span of time. Perry cannot explain either the repetition of Jesus' appearances nor the time span over which He appeared.

3. *Veridical visions cannot explain the physical, bodily nature of Jesus' appearances.* Veridical visions are mental projections. They are not physical appearances nor do they leave physical effects. The resurrection appearances, however, were physical and bodily, as we have seen. A veridical vision only looks real—it cannot break bread or be grasped by the feet or eat food, such as occurred in Jesus' appearances. After a veridical vision is past, everything remains undisturbed as it was before. Hence, the disciples could not have mistaken a veridical vision for a real appearance of Jesus. It is interesting to note that during Jesus' time, the Jews distinguished between a vision and an appearance of an angel precisely on this basis: if the food seen to be eaten by the angel was left undisturbed, then the angel was just a vision; but if the food had been consumed, then the angel had actually appeared. With that in mind, we can see that the disciples could not have mistakenly taken a vision of Jesus for an appearance, for the basis of discriminating between a vision and an appearance was their physical reality. At any rate, the physicalism of Jesus' appearances is well established and thus precludes their being mere veridical visions.

4. *Veridical visions of dead persons only occur to individuals who are unaware of the person's death.* The casebooks show that people who have veridical visions are not aware that the person seen has died. That consideration seems to be decisive against this theory. For the disciples not only knew of Jesus' death; they were shattered by it. Therefore, they could not have been subject to a veridical vision.

5. *The hypothesis fails to account for all the evidence.* Again we find a familiar problem: the theory seeks to explain part of the evidence, but leaves other important aspects unexplained. Many additional theories would need to be added in order to account for the full range of the data. The empty tomb would have to be accounted for by some unrelated hypothesis. The

appearance to the five hundred would have to be explained as a mere hallucination, not a veridical vision, Perry admits, since too many people were involved. The appearance to Paul would also have to be explained as a coincidental hallucination, not a veridical vision, Perry acknowledges, presumably because Paul lacked the intimate contact with Jesus necessary for a veridical vision. Thus, multiple hypotheses, against which weighty objections could be lodged, are necessary to account for the evidence that the single, overarching hypothesis of the resurrection plausibly explains. Historically, therefore, the explanation that Jesus rose from the dead is to be preferred.

In summary, we have examined in detail four lines of historical evidence concerning the appearances of Jesus after His death. Those demonstrate that Jesus on several occasions and in different places appeared physically and bodily alive from the dead to His followers, to His brother, and to Paul. Neither hallucinations nor veridical visions provide an adequate explanation of those appearances. On this basis alone, we would be justified in concluding that Jesus rose from the dead, as the disciples proclaimed. But all the evidence for the resurrection is not yet in: we still have to consider the evidence for the origin of the Christian faith. So before we draw any final conclusion, let us turn to the next chapter to consider the question, How is the origin of the Christian faith to be explained?

NOTES

1. C. H. Dodd, "The Appearances of the Risen Christ: A study in the form criticism of the Gospels," in *More New Testament Studies* (Manchester: U. of Manchester Press, 1968), p. 128.
2. Josephus *Jewish War* 3. 41-43.
3. Josephus *Antiquities of the Jews* 20. 200. There is also an account by Hegesippus recorded in Eusebius *Historiae ecclesiasticae* 2. 33.
4. Eusebius *Historiae ecclesiasticae* 1. 7, 14.

5. Hans Grass, *Ostergeschehen und Osterberichte*, 4th ed. (Göttingen: Vandenhoeck & Ruprecht, 1970), p. 102.

6. Indeed, so strong is the evidence for these appearances that Wolfhart Pannenberg, perhaps the world's greatest living systematic theologian, has rocked modern, skeptical German theology by building his entire theology precisely on the historical evidence for the resurrection of Jesus as supplied in Paul's list of appearances (Wolfhart Pannenberg, *Jesus: God and Man*, trans. L. L. Wilkins and D. A. Priebe [London: SCM, 1968], pp. 88-99.) Pannenberg also argues for the empty tomb, but its role in his case is subsidiary and confirmatory.

7. Julius Müller, *The Theory of Myths, in its Application to the Gospel History, Examined and Confuted* (London: John Chapman, 1844), p. 26.

8. A. N. Sherwin-White, *Roman Society and Roman Law in the New Testament* (Oxford: Clarendon, 1963), pp. 188-91.

9. Ibid., p. 189.

10. Ibid., p. 190.

11. Müller, *Theory*, p. 29.

12. John A. T. Robinson, *Redating the New Testament* (London: SCM, 1976), pp. 3, 342-48.

13. Bo Reicke, "Synoptic Prophecies on the Destruction of Jerusalem," in *Studies in New Testament and Early Christian Literature*, ed. D. E. Aune (Leiden: E. J. Brill, 1972), pp. 121-34.

14. Robinson, *Redating*, p. 343.

15. Donald Guthrie, *New Testament Introduction*, 3d ed. rev. (London: Inter-Varsity, 1970), pp. 340-45.

16. Vincent Taylor, *The Formation of the Gospel Tradition*, 2d ed. (London: Macmillan, 1935), p. 41.

17. Walther Künneth, *The Theology of the Resurrection*, trans. J. W. Leitch (London: SCM, 1965), pp. 92-93.

18. Ibid., p. 93.

19. Jean Héring, *La première épître de saint Paul aux Corinthiens*, 2d ed., Commentaire du Nouveau Testament 7 (Neuchatel, Switzerland: Delachaux et Niestlé, 1959), p. 147.

20. Grass, *Ostergeschehen*, pp. 229-32.

21. E. E. Ellis, ed, *The Gospel of Luke*, New Century Bible (London: Nelson, 1966), p. 275.

22. Irenaeus *Against Heresies* 1. 26. 1.

23. Rudolf Schnackenburg, *Das Johannesevangelium*, 2d ed., 3 vols.,

Herders theologischer Kommentar zum Neuen Testament 4 (Freiburg: Herder, 1972-76), 3: 383.

24. Michael Perry, *The Easter Enigma* (London: Faber & Faber, 1959), pp. 141-95.

25. Ibid., p. 214.

5

The Origin of the Christian Faith

Whatever they may think of the historical resurrection, even the most skeptical scholars admit that at least the *belief* that Jesus rose from the dead lay at the very heart of the earliest Christian faith. Bultmann, though he denies the historical resurrection, yet acknowledges that historical criticism can establish that the first disciples believed in the resurrection.[1] Gerhard Koch states, "It is everywhere clear that the event of Easter is the central point of the New Testament message. Resurrection by God and appearing before his disciples constitute the basis of the New Testament proclamation of Christ, without which there would be virtually no witness to Christ."[2] When Paul wrote, "If Christ has not been raised, then our preaching is vain, your faith also is in vain" (1 Corinthians 15:14), he was not giving just his own opinion. The entire New Testament testifies to the fact that the resurrection of Jesus stood at the center of the disciples' faith and preaching.

It was on the basis of Jesus' resurrection that the disciples could believe that He was the Messiah. It is difficult to exaggerate how devastating the crucifixion must have been for the disciples. They had pinned all their hopes, their lives, on Jesus, but He had died. Even though Jesus had predicted his resurrection, the gospels are clear that the disciples did not understand Him. They had no conception of a dying, much less a rising, Messiah, for the Scriptures said that the Messiah would reign forever (Isaiah 9:7; compare John 12:34). Thus, Jesus' crucifixion shattered any hopes they might have entertained that He was the Messiah.

127

But the resurrection turned catastrophe into victory. Because God had raised Jesus from the dead, He was proved to be the Messiah after all. In Acts 2:32, 36, Peter declares to the Jews, "This Jesus God raised up. . . . Let all the house of Israel know for certain that God has made Him both Lord and Christ, this Jesus whom you crucified." "Christ" was the Greek word for "Messiah," and it became so closely connected to Jesus' person that it became practically a proper name: Messiah Jesus became Jesus Christ. The resurrection was God's decisive vindication of who Jesus was. It showed that the crucifixion was no defeat, but part of God's plan. Belief in the resurrection enabled the disciples to proclaim that their crucified Master was the Messiah of God.

The resurrection was also central to salvation from sins. Paul writes that Jesus "was delivered up because of our transgressions, and was raised because of our justification" (Romans 4:24-25). On the basis of the resurrection, Peter could proclaim, "Every one who believes in Him receives forgiveness of sins" (Acts 10:43). Belief in Jesus' resurrection was therefore one of the necessary conditions for salvation. An early confession cited by Paul states: "If you confess with your mouth Jesus as Lord, and believe in your heart that God raised Him from the dead, you shall be saved" (Romans 10:9). Apart from belief in the resurrection, there could be no salvation or forgiveness of sins. Without the resurrection, the cross would have no meaning. This is why Paul could write, "If Christ has not been raised, your faith is worthless; you are still in your sins" (1 Corinthians 15:17).

It is quite clear that without the belief in the resurrection the Christian faith could not have come into being. The disciples would have remained crushed and defeated men. Even had they continued to remember Jesus as their beloved teacher, His crucifixion would have forever silenced any hopes of His being the Messiah. The cross would have remained the sad and shameful end to His career. *The origin of Christianity therefore hinges on the belief of the early disciples that God had raised Jesus from the dead.*

Now the question becomes: What caused that belief? As R. H. Fuller says, even the most skeptical critic must presuppose some mysterious x to get the movement going.[3] But what was that x?

If one denies that Jesus really did rise from the dead, then he must explain the disciples' belief that He did rise either in terms of Jewish influences or in terms of Christian influences. Clearly, it could not be the result of Christian influences, for at that time there was no Christianity. Since belief in Jesus' resurrection was the foundation for the origin of the Christian faith, it cannot be a belief formed as a result of that faith.

But neither can belief in the resurrection be explained as a result of Jewish influences. To see that we must turn to the Old Testament. Resurrection of the dead on the day of judgment is mentioned in three places (Ezekiel 37; Isaiah 26:19; Daniel 12:2). During the time between the Old Testament and the New Testament, the belief in resurrection flowered and is often mentioned in the Jewish literature of that period. In Jesus' day the Jewish party of the Pharisees held to belief in resurrection, and Jesus sided with them on that score in opposition to the party of the Sadducees. So the idea of resurrection was itself nothing new.

But the Jewish conception of resurrection differed in two important, fundamental respects from Jesus' resurrection. In Jewish thought the resurrection *always* (1) occurred after the end of the world, not within history, and (2) concerned all the people, not just an isolated individual. In contradistinction to this, Jesus' resurrection was both within history and of one person.

With regard to the first point, the Jewish belief was always that at the end of history God would raise the dead and receive them into heaven. There are, to be sure, examples in the Old Testament of *resuscitations* of the dead; but the persons would die again. The resurrection to eternal life and glory only occurred after the end of the world. We find that

Jewish outlook in the gospels themselves. Thus, when Jesus assured Martha that her brother Lazarus would rise again, she responded, "I know that he will rise again in the resurrection at the last day" (John 11:24). She had no idea that Jesus was about to bring him back to life. Similarly, when Jesus told His disciples that He would rise from the dead, they thought he meant at the end of the world (Mark 9:9-13). The idea that a true resurrection could occur prior to God's bringing the kingdom of heaven at the end of the world was utterly foreign to them. The greatly renowned German New Testament scholar Joachim Jeremias writes:

> Ancient Judaism did not know of an anticipated resurrection as an event of history. Nowhere does one find in the literature anything comparable to the resurrection of Jesus. Certainly resurrections of the dead were known, but these always concerned resuscitations, the return to the earthly life. In no place in the late Judaic literature does it concern a resurrection to δόξα [glory] as an event of history.[4]

The disciples, therefore, confronted with Jesus' crucifixion and death, would only have looked forward to the resurrection at the final day and would probably have carefully kept their master's tomb as a shrine, where His bones could reside until the resurrection. They would not have come up with the idea that he was already raised.

As for the second point, the Jewish idea of resurrection was always of a general resurrection of the dead, not an isolated individual. It was the people, or mankind as a whole, that God raised up in the resurrection. But in Jesus' resurrection, God raised just a single man. Moreover, there was no concept of the people's resurrection in some way hinging on the Messiah's resurrection. That was just totally unknown. Yet that is precisely what is said to have occurred in Jesus' case. Ulrich Wilckens, another prominent German New Testament critic, explains:

> For nowhere do the Jewish texts speak of the resurrection of an

individual which already occurs before the resurrection of the righteous in the end time and is differentiated and separate from it; nowhere does the participation of the righteous in the salvation at the end time depend on their belonging to the Messiah, who was raised in advance as the 'First of those raised by God.' [1 Corinthians 15:20][5]

It is therefore evident that the disciples would not as a result of Jewish influences or background come up with the idea that Jesus alone had been raised from the dead. They would wait with longing for that day when He and all the righteous of Israel would be raised by God to glory.

The disciples' belief in Jesus' resurrection, therefore, cannot be explained as the result of either Christian or Jewish influences. Left to themselves, the disciples would never have come up with such an idea as Jesus' resurrection. And remember: they were fishermen and taxcollectors, not theologians. The mysterious x is still missing. According to C. F. D. Moule of Cambridge University, here is a belief nothing in terms of previous historical influences can account for.[6] He points out that we have a situation in which a large number of people held firmly to this belief, which cannot be explained in terms of the Old Testament or the Pharisees, and that these people held onto this belief until the Jews finally threw them out of the synagogue. According to Professor Moule, the origin of this belief must have been the fact that Jesus really did rise from the dead:

> If the coming into existence of the Nazarenes, a phenomenon undeniably attested by the New Testament, rips a great hole in history, a hole of the size and shape of the Resurrection, what does the secular historian propose to stop it up with? . . . the birth and rapid rise of the Christian Church . . . *remain an unsolved enigma for any historian who refuses to take seriously the only explanation offered by the Church itself.*[7]

The resurrection of Jesus is therefore the best explanation for the origin of the Christian faith.

But suppose the disciples were not just "left to themselves." Suppose certain events led them to think that Jesus was risen from the dead. Let us assume, for example, that shock at finding Jesus' tomb empty caused them to see hallucinations of Jesus alive from the dead. Could not that lead them to conclude that Jesus had been resurrected? Of course, you will probably think at this point, "But those hypotheses have already been extensively refuted and shown to be worthless." But let us be generous and overlook all that we have said before. The question is, *If* that happened, would the disciples have proclaimed that Jesus was risen from the dead?

The answer is no, since hallucinations, as projections of the mind, can contain nothing new. But Jesus' resurrection involved at least two radically new aspects not found in Jewish belief: it was a resurrection in history, not at the end of history, and it was the resurrection of an isolated individual, not of the whole people. Even if it were possible, therefore, that the disciples under the influence of the empty tomb projected hallucinatory visions of Jesus, they would never have projected Him as literally risen from the dead. They would have had a vision of Jesus in glory in Abraham's bosom. That is where, in Jewish belief, the souls of the righteous go to await the final resurrection. If the disciples were to have visions, then they would have seen Jesus there in glory.

They never would have come to the idea that Jesus had been resurrected from the dead. Even finding the empty tomb, the disciples would have concluded only that Jesus had been "translated" or "taken up" directly to heaven. In the Old Testament both Enoch (Genesis 5:24; Hebrews 11:5) and Elijah (2 Kings 2:11-18) were supposed to have been translated to heaven. Stories of persons being translated to heaven are also found in Jewish writings outside the Bible (for example, Testament of Job 40, where the bodies of two children killed in the collapse of a house are not found, but later the children are seen glorified in heaven). It cannot be emphasized strongly enough that, for the Jew, a translation and a resurrection are two entirely different things. A translation is the taking up of a person directly into heaven. A resurrection is the physical and bodily raising up of the dead man in the tomb to new life. Therefore, if the disciples did see hallucinatory visions of Jesus, then even with the empty tomb, they would never have concluded that He had been raised from the dead, an idea that ran contrary to Jewish concepts of the resurrection; rather they would have concluded that God had translated Him into heaven, from where He appeared to them, and therefore the tomb was empty. The fact that the disciples proclaimed not the translation of Jesus, as with Enoch and Elijah, but—contrary to all Jewish concepts—the resurrection of Jesus, proves that the origin of the disciples' belief in Jesus' resurrection cannot be explained as their conclusion from the empty tomb and visions.

Therefore, even apart from the improbabilities of those hypotheses, it is clear that the empty tomb/hallucination explanation of the origin of the belief in Jesus' resurrection is untenable. There is no way to explain the origin of the disciples' belief that Jesus had been raised from the dead apart from the fact that He really was raised.

In summary, we have seen that the origin of the Christian faith owes itself to the belief of the earliest disciples that Jesus had been raised from the dead. But the origin of that belief itself cannot be explained either in terms of Christian or Jewish influences. Moreover, even if we grant for the sake of argument the hypotheses already refuted in themselves that the empty tomb was the result of theft and the appearances were hallucinations, the origin of the belief in Jesus' resurrection still cannot be explained, for such phenomena would have led the disciples to conclude only that Jesus had been translated, not resurrected. Therefore, the origin of the belief in Jesus' resurrection and thereby the origin of the Christian faith itself can only be plausibly explained if in fact Jesus actually rose from the dead.

Now we are ready to draw the conclusion that we have so

long postponed. First, we have seen that ten lines of historical evidence support the fact that Jesus' tomb was found empty. We further saw that no natural explanation has been offered that can plausibly account for the empty tomb. Second, we have also seen that four lines of historical evidence support the fact that on numerous occasions and in different places Jesus appeared bodily and physically alive from the dead to different witnesses. We found that no natural explanation, either in terms of hallucinations or veridical visions, could plausibly account for those appearances. Finally, we have seen that the very origin of the Christian faith depends on the belief in Jesus' resurrection and that this belief cannot be plausibly explained in terms of natural causes. Each of these three great facts—the empty tomb, the appearances, the origin of the Christian faith—is independently established. Together they point with unwavering conviction to the same unavoidable and marvelous conclusion: *Jesus actually rose from the dead.*

NOTES

1. Rudolph Bultmann, "New Testament and Mythology," in *Kerygma and Myth,* ed. Hans Werner Bartsch, trans. R. H. Fuller, 2 vols. (London: SPCK, 1953), 1:42.
2. Gerhard Koch, *Die Auferstehung Jesu Christi,* Beiträge zur historischen Theologie (Tübingen: J. C. B. Mohr, 1959), p. 25.
3. R. H. Fuller, *The Formation of the Resurrection Narratives* (London: SPCK, 1972), p. 2.
4. Joachim Jeremias, "Die älteste Schicht der Osterüberlieferung," in *Resurrexit,* ed. Édouard Dhanis (Rome: Libreria Editrice Vaticana, 1974), p. 194.
5. Ulrich Wilckens, *Auferstehung,* Themen der Theologie 4 (Stuttgart and Berlin: Kreuz Verlag, 1970), p. 131.
6. C. F. D. Moule and Don Cupitt, "The Resurrection: A Disagreement," *Theology* 75 (1972): 507-19.
7. C. F. D. Moule, *The Phenomenon of the New Testament,* Studies in Biblical Theology 2/1 (London: SCM, 1967), pp. 3, 13.

6

Finding Resurrection Life

"There ain't gonna be no Easter this year," a student friend remarked to me.

"Why not?" I asked incredulously.

"They found the body."

Despite his irreverent humor, my friend displayed a measure of insight often not shared by modern theologians. His joke correctly perceived that without the resurrection Christianity is worthless.

The earliest Christians would certainly have agreed with my friend. The apostle Paul put it straight and simple: "If Christ was not raised then neither our preaching nor your faith has any meaning at all. . . . If Christ did not rise your faith is futile and your sins have never been forgiven" (1 Corinthians 15:14, 17, Phillips). For the earliest Christians, Jesus' resurrection was a historical fact, every bit as real as His death on the cross. Without the resurrection, Christianity would have been simply false. Jesus would have been just another prophet who had met His unfortunate fate at the hands of the Jews. Faith in Him as Lord, Messiah, or Son of God would have been stupid. There would be no use in trying to save the situation by interpreting the resurrection as some sort of symbol. The cold, hard facts of reality would remain: Jesus was dead and anything He started died with him.

David C. K. Watson tells the true story of another man who understood this, with tragic consequences.[1] The man was a retired clergyman who in his spare time began to study the thought of certain modern theologians on the resurrection. He read books on the resurrection and watched television talk shows on the subject. In his old age, he felt sure that the highly educated professors and writers knew

135

far more than he did and that they were surely right when they said Jesus had not literally risen from the dead. He understood clearly what that meant for him: his whole life and ministry had been based on a bundle of lies. He committed suicide.

I believe that modern theologians must answer to God for that man's death. One cannot make statements on such matters without accepting part of the responsibility for the consequences. The average layman probably expects that theologians would be biased in favor of the resurrection, when in fact exactly the opposite is often true. It has not been historians who have denied the historical resurrection of Jesus, but theologians. Why this strange situation? According to Carl Braaten, theologians who deny the resurrection have not done so on historical grounds; rather, theology has been derailed by existentialism and historicism, which have a stranglehold on the formation of theological statements.[2] Hence, the statements of many theologians concerning the resurrection of Jesus actually are not based on fact, but are determined by philosophical assumptions. That makes statements that deny that Jesus' resurrection was a historical fact all the more irresponsible, for their conclusion has not been determined by the facts, which support the historicity of the resurrection, but by assumptions.

The point is that the Christian faith stands or falls with the resurrection of Jesus. It is no use saying, as some theologians do, "We believe in the risen Christ, not in the empty tomb!" For as has often been pointed out, one cannot really believe in the risen Christ without the empty tomb. So let us have no talk of the resurrection's being false but having value as a symbol. If Jesus did not rise from the dead, then He was a tragedy and a failure, and no amount of theologizing or symbolizing could change the situation. My student friend was right: without the resurrection there would be no Easter. As Gerald O'Collins puts it, "In a profound sense, Christianity without the resurrection is not simply Christianity without its final chapter. It is not Christianity at all."[3]

But we have seen that the historical evidence supports the resurrection of Jesus. The empty tomb, the resurrection appearances, and the origin of the Christian faith can be explained only if Jesus actually rose from the dead. This amazing fact has three profound consequences for us today:

1. *The resurrection of Jesus was an act of God.* In order to see that, it is important for us to remind ourselves of exactly what Jesus' resurrection was. For Jesus' resurrection was not just a resuscitation of the mortal body to this earthly life, as with Lazarus, miraculous as that would be. Rather Jesus rose to eternal life in a radically transformed body that could be described as immortal, glorious, powerful, and supernatural. In that new mode of existence, He was not bound by the physical limitations of this universe, but possessed superhuman powers. The disciples proclaimed the resurrection as an act of God: "This Jesus God raised up, to which we are all witnesses" (Acts 2:32). *Anyone who denies this explanation is rationally obligated to produce a more plausible cause of Jesus' resurrection and to explain how it happened.* It is not enough for a skeptic glibly to assert that there might have been some cause of the resurrection other than God; rather he must name that cause, and explain its operation in this unique instance. For the resurrection of Jesus so far exceeds the causal power of nature that nothing that we have learned in the two thousand years that have elapsed since that remarkable event enables us to account for its occurrence. Most men recognize this truth, as is evident from the fact that those who have opposed the resurrection have always tried to explain away the facts without admitting that Jesus was raised. Once it is admitted that Jesus really did rise transformed from the dead, the conclusion that God raised Him up is virtually inescapable. Only a sterile, academic skepticism resists this inevitable inference.

2. *The resurrection of Jesus confirms His personal claims.* Jesus' resurrection did not occur at an accidental point in history. Rather it came in the context of and as the climax to His life and ministry. Jesus, even humanly speaking, was an

incredible person.[4] He evidently thought of Himself as being the Son of God in a unique sense. That is seen in His prayer life. Jesus addressed God in prayer as "Abba," the word a Jewish child used for "Papa." For a Jew the very name of God was sacred, and no one would dare to address God in such a for one's teaching. But Jesus did exactly the opposite. He to His heavenly Father as "Papa." He taught His disciples to pray, "Our Father." But he always prayed, "My Father." God was Jesus' Father in a distinctive sense that set Him apart from the disciples.

Jesus' special sense of being God's Son is evident in His words "Everything has been put into my hands by my Father, and nobody knows the Son except the Father. Nor does anyone know the Father except the Son—and the man to whom the Son chooses to reveal him" (Matthew 11:27, Phillips). This is a claim to sonship in an exclusive and absolute sense. The relationship between Jesus and His Father is here declared to be unique. Jesus also claims to be the *only one* who can reveal the Father to men; in other words, Jesus claims to be the absolute revelation of God.

Jesus not only claimed to be God's Son in a unique sense, but He also claimed to act and speak with divine authority. That is especially evident in the Sermon on the Mount. The typical rabbinic style of teaching was to quote extensively from learned teachers who provided the basis of authority for one's teaching. But Jesus did exactly the opposite. He began, "You have heard that it was said to the men of old" (Matthew 5:33, RSV) then quoted some interpretation of the law of Moses. Then he continued (5:34) "But I say to you," and gave His own teaching. No wonder that Matthew comments, "When Jesus finished these sayings, the crowds were astonished at His teaching, for He taught them as one who had authority, and not as their scribes" (Matthew 7:28-29, RSV). Jesus' special sense of authority is also evident in His use of the expression "Truly, truly, I say to you," which He used as an introduction to His authoritative word on some subject.

His authority was also evident in His role as an exorcist. It is an embarrassment to many modern theologians, but it is historically certain that Jesus believed He had the power to cast out demons. That was a sign to the people of his divine authority. He said, "If it is by the finger of God that I cast out demons, then the Kingdom of God has come upon you" (Luke 11:20, RSV). That saying is remarkable not only because it shows He claimed divine authority over the spiritual powers of evil, but also because it shows that Jesus believed that in Himself the kingdom of God had come. The Jews believed that the kingdom of God would come at the end of history when the Messiah would reign over Israel and the nations. But Jesus was saying, "My ability to rule the spiritual forces of darkness shows that in Me the kingdom of God is already present among you."

We can also see Jesus' consciousness of authority in His claim to be able to forgive sins. We find such a claim, for example, in the context of a healing miracle related by Mark. "[I will] prove to you that the Son of Man has full authority to forgive sins on earth" (Mark 2:10, Phillips). Such a claim is remarkable when one considers the Jewish belief that only God could forgive sins. Mark relates, "Some of the scribes were sitting there silently asking themselves, 'Why does this man talk such blasphemy? Who can forgive sins but God alone?'" (Mark 2:6-7, Phillips). Jesus' claim was thus a claim to an authority held only by God.

Jesus also believed Himself to be able to work miracles. Jesus said to the disciples of John the Baptist, "Go and tell John what you hear and see; the blind receive their sight and the lame walk, lepers are cleansed and the deaf hear, and the dead are raised up, and the poor have the good news preached to them" (Matthew 11:4-5, RSV). James D. G. Dunn comments on this saying: "Whatever the 'facts' were, Jesus evidently believed that he had cured cases of blindness, lameness and deafness—indeed there is no reason to doubt that He believed lepers had been cured under His ministry and dead restored to life."[5] One might go on to argue that

Jesus could surely not have been mistaken about such palpable facts as these, but that is not the issue at hand. The point is simply that Jesus at least thought he had the power to perform miracles.

Finally, Jesus held that men's attitudes toward Himself would be the determining factor in God's judgment on the judgment day. "I tell you, everyone who acknowledges me before men, the Son of man also will acknowledge before the angels of God; but he who denies me before men will be denied before the angels of God" (Luke 12:8-9, RSV). "Son of Man" is often thought to indicate the humanity of Jesus, just as the reflex expression "Son of God" indicates His divinity. In fact, just the opposite is true. The Son of Man was a divine figure in the Old Testament book of Daniel who would come at the end of the world to judge mankind and rule forever. Thus, the claim to be the Son of Man would be in effect a claim to divinity. I have no doubt that in this passage Jesus is not referring to a third figure as the Son of Man, but is referring to Himself by means of that title. That is, however, for the moment beside the point. The point is that whoever the Son of Man may be, Jesus is claiming that men will be judged before Him on the basis of their response to Jesus. Men's eternal destiny is fixed on their response to Jesus. Make no mistake: if Jesus were not the divine Son of God, then this claim could only be regarded as the most narrow and objectionable dogmatism. For Jesus is saying that men's salvation depends on their confession to Jesus Himself.

A discussion of Jesus' personal claims could go on and on, but I think this is sufficient to indicate the radical self-concept of Jesus. Here is a man who thought of Himself as the Son of God in a unique sense, who claimed to act and speak with divine authority, who held Himself to be a worker of miracles, and who believed that men's eternal destiny hinged on whether or not they believed in Him. So extraordinary was the person Jesus thought Himself to be that Dunn, at the end of his study of the self-consciousness ot Jesus, feels compelled to remark: "One last question cannot be ignored: *Was Jesus mad?*"[6]

Dunn rejects the hypothesis that Jesus was insane because it cannot account for the full portrait of Jesus that we have in the gospels. The balance and soundness of Jesus' whole life make it evident that He was no lunatic. But the decisive disproof of this hypothesis is, of course, the resurrection. *The resurrection vindicates the claims that Jesus made concerning himself.* Wolfhart Pannenberg explains,

> The resurrection of Jesus acquires such decisive meaning, not merely because someone or any one has been raised from the dead, but because it is Jesus of Nazareth, whose execution was instigated by the Jews because he had blasphemed against God. If this man was raised from the dead, then that plainly means that the God whom he had supposedly blasphemed has committed himself to him.[7]

Pannenberg points out that the key element in Jesus' teaching was Jesus' personal claim to authority, evident in His handling of the Mosaic law and His preaching of the dawning of the kingdom of God. It was this claim that led to His execution for blasphemy by the Jews. But His resurrection showed that Jesus' claim was justified. "The resurrection can only be understood as the divine vindication of the man whom the Jews had rejected as a blasphemer."[8] Therefore, the resurrection shows that Jesus, in making those astounding personal claims was not mad, but really was who He claimed to be.

3. *The resurrection of Jesus shows that He holds the key to eternal life.* As the one who decisively conquered death, Jesus is the one to whom we must turn for victory over man's most dreaded enemy. On the subject of death and immortality, Jesus spoke with the authority of the victor over death. In this light His dispute with the Sadducees becomes very important. The Sadducees were a Jewish sect that denied there was any future resurrection life and concocted puzzles designed to show its impossibility. For example, suppose a

woman was widowed and remarried seven times in this life.
In the resurrection, who out of the seven husbands will have
her for his wife? The Sadducees posed that question to Jesus,
and Mark recorded what He said:

> Jesus replied, "Does not this show where you go wrong—and
> how you fail to understand both the scriptures and the power of
> God? When people rise from the dead they neither marry nor
> are they given in marriage; they live like the angels in Heaven.
> But as for this matter of the dead being raised, have you never
> read in the book of Moses, in the passage about the bush, how
> God spoke to him in these words, 'I am the God of Abraham and
> the God of Isaac and the God of Jacob'? God is not God of the
> dead but of living men! That is where you make your great
> mistake!" [Mark 12:24-27, Phillips]

Jesus could not have been more clear or emphatic. He held
that the Old Testament Scriptures teach immortality through
resurrection, and He believed it himself. He rebuked the
Sadducees for their ignorance of Scripture and their limited
conception of God's power, as evident in their puzzle. As for
Jesus' solution, He may mean simply that in the same way
that angels are not married, neither will people in the
resurrection life be married. But He may also mean that
people will be like the angels in heaven physically. The
descriptions of Jesus' resurrection body in the gospels
coincide closely with biblical descriptions of angels. Angels,
too, can appear and disappear in space. When they appear,
they are really physically present. Though they are created
beings they are immortal. They are often described as
glorious, and they possess superhuman powers. Thus, there
is a great resemblance between angelic bodies and Jesus'
resurrection body. That does not mean that people become
angels when they die, as is often mistakenly pictured in
cartoons of people receiving their harps and wings. According to the Bible, angels are a separate order of beings higher
than man. Jesus said that in the resurrection people would
be *like* angels. If he means physically like angels, then his
teaching is very similar to Paul's teaching on the resurrection

body as immortal, glorious, powerful, and supernatural.

Jesus' teaching therefore holds out hope for man in the face of death. The grave is not the end. At history's end we shall be raised up by God and simultaneously transformed into persons having glorious, supernatural bodies. We shall never again experience disease or deformity or aging. We shall have powers that the present body in no way possesses. We shall apparently overcome the limits of space, so that travel from one point to another may be accomplished instantaneously. At the same time we shall still be ourselves, as recognizable to others as Jesus was to His disciples after His resurrection. Evil will be gone, along with all the ugly sins that men have committed against one another. And death will be forever vanquished, never again to hold sway over man. What a wonderful prospect! What a hope! That is what Paul so magnificently describes:

> Lo! I tell you a mystery. We shall not all sleep, but we shall all be changed, in a moment, in the twinkling of an eye, at the last trumpet. For the trumpet will sound, and the dead will be raised imperishable, and we shall be changed. For this perishable nature must put on the imperishable, and this mortal nature must put on immortality. When the perishable puts on the imperishable, and the mortal puts on immortality, then shall come to pass the saying that is written:
> "Death is swallowed up in victory."
> "O death, where is thy victory?
> O death, where is thy sting?"
> The sting of death is sin, and the power of sin is the law. But thanks be to God, who gives us the victory through our Lord Jesus Christ." [1 Corinthians 15:51-57, RSV]

Thus the resurrection of Jesus offers to man both God and immortality. It is almost too wonderful, too incredible to believe. But the facts are there. God has revealed Himself in history, and the evidence is there for all to see.

But the question now becomes, How am I to appropriate the immortal life God offers? In order to answer that question, I want to share with you by means of four points the message proclaimed by the New Testament Christians.

1. *God loves you and created you to have a personal relationship with him.* Man is not the accidental product of nature. Rather God created man to be a personal being, just as God is personal. In that way man could know and commune with God. John reports the words of Jesus in prayer to the Father: "And this is eternal life, to know you, the only true God, and him whom you have sent—Jesus Christ" (John 17:3, Phillips). What a striking definition of eternal life! *Eternal life is knowing God.* That is why God created us as persons: that we might have a personal love relationship with Him.

2. *Man's own evil has broken the personal relationship between God and man.* In creating man as a free personal being, God took a terrible risk. Man might freely choose to reject God's love and not to have a personal relationship with Him. God could have made man like a puppet, so that when God asked, "Do you love me?" all He had to do was pull the appropriate strings and man would mechanically respond, "Yes, God, I love you." But what sort of personal relationship is that? Love must be freely given to be meaningful. But that, as I say, involves the risk of being rejected. And that is exactly what has happened. Man freely chooses to go his own way and commits evil acts and thoughts that are contrary to the absolute goodness of God. The Bible indicates that all men have succumbed to and are therefore under the sway of such evil. If any biblical truth has been proved by the experience of mankind, it is certainly the fact of evil in man. There are at least three terrible consequences of that fact.

a) *Man stands morally guilty before God.* What man has done is *really* evil, for it goes contrary to the very nature of God. God's nature is absolute goodness, so that before Him man is morally guilty. To be sure, some are more guilty than others. But it is only a matter of degree, since no man reaches the moral perfection of God's nature. Therefore, all men are accountable to God for their evil thoughts and deeds and must be punished. If God did not punish evil, then He would not be all-good, for His justice would be flawed. Before the bar of God's perfect justice, man stands condemned as morally guilty.

b) Man's personal relationship with God is broken. "God is light and in him is no darkness at all" (1 John 1:5). And just as light dispels darkness, so the light of God's absolute goodness dispels the darkness of evil from His presence. Man in his sinful state cannot have a personal relationship with God. The prophet Isaiah said:

> Behold, the Lord's hand is not shortened, that it cannot save, or his ear dull, that it cannot hear;
> but your iniquities have made a separation between you and your God,
> and your sins have hid his face from you so that he does not hear.
> Isaiah 59:1-2, RSV

Because man is stained with evil, his personal relationship with God is broken. Hence, Paul could write, "Everyone has sinned, everyone falls short of the beauty of God's plan" (Romans 3:23, Phillips).

Man senses in this condition that he is lost and often tries to get back to God by his own efforts. He invents religions, develops philosophies, meditates, takes drugs, or chooses any one of a number of other avenues to reach God, but in vain. For none of those self-his being by separates man from God. Were man to die in this state, he would go into eternity forever cut off from God. This is really what the New Testament means by "hell." Paul warned, "This judgment . . . will bring full justice in dazzling flame upon those who have refused to recognise God or to obey the gospel of our Lord Jesus. Their punishment will be eternal loss—exclusion from the radiance of the face of the Lord, and the glorious majesty of his power" (2 Thessalonians 1:8-9, Phillips). Thus the separation from God brought about as a result of man's evil destroys any personal relationship with God, which man was created to have.

c) Man is spiritually dead. Morally guilty and separated from God, man is spiritually dead. Paul reminded the Christians at Ephesus, "You were [spiritually] dead in your trespasses and sins" (Ephesians 2:1). Man is like a light bulb with a burned out filament. Externally he may look fine, but internally he is defective. That aspect of his being by which he should know God is rendered inoperative and dead because of his evil.

Thus, man stands morally guilty before God. His personal relationship with God is broken, and he is spiritually dead. If this were all the Bible had to say to us, it would be bad news indeed.

3. *Through Jesus man's personal relationship with God is restored.* We have already said that in creating man as a free personal being, God was running the risk that man would turn away from Him. That in fact has happened. As a result, God puts Himself in a moral dilemma: on the one hand, God's goodness and justice demand that man be punished for his evil, but on the other hand, God's love and mercy demand reconciliation of man to God. God's goodness demands punishment and God's love demands forgiveness. Neither can be compromised. What is God to do? Now I do not mean to imply that God has unwittingly got Himself into this situation. God is all-knowing. Before the creation of the universe He knew that the man He would create would go astray, and that this dilemma would arise as a result. But He also knew what He would do to solve it.

What God has done reveals His genius. *He Himself became a man, lived a sinless life, and died in man's place to pay the penalty for man's sins.* Now when the New Testament says that God in Jesus took the form of a man, it does not refer to the sort of transformation by which the gods of Greek mythology turned into swans, bulls, men, or whatever. The incarnation does not hold that God somehow turned into a man, which is self-contradictory. Rather, in Jesus God took on a human body without at the same time ceasing to be God. Jesus was thus both God and man *simultaneously*. That is, the mind of

Jesus was God. Jesus of Nazareth was thus the unique Son of God, the God-man. John wrote:

> At the beginning God expressed himself. That personal expression, that word, was with God and was God. . . . So the word of God became a human being and lived among us. We saw his glory (the glory like that of a father's only son), full of grace and truth. . . . It is true that no one has ever seen God at any time. Yet the divine and only Son, who lives in the closest intimacy with the Father, has made him known. [John 1:1, 14, 18, Phillips]

Jesus did what no man had yet done: He lived a sinless life. This meant that He was therefore not morally guilty before God and not obligated to be punished for sin. Because of that, only Jesus could offer Himself voluntarily to be punished for someone else's sin. That He did on the cross. There He took upon Himself, the sinless Son of God, the punishment for all the billions and billions of sins ever committed by all the billions of people who ever have lived and ever will live. That is why in the Garden of Gethsemane prior to His crucifixion Jesus prayed to God with tears and loud cries. It was not that He feared the physical suffering, gruesome as that was; it was the knowledge that He was about to be punished for the sins of the world that shook Him to the core. While Jesus was on the cross, the Father turned His back, as it were, on His Son, and He who had never known separation from the Father went through hell for us. At the cross, therefore, we see the fulfillment of God's justice *and* love. We see God's justice in His punishment of sin. We see His love in that He does not punish us for our sins as we deserve; but rather in Jesus He Himself pays the penalty He had exacted. That is why Paul could exclaim, "The proof of God's amazing love is this: that it was *while we were sinners* that Christ died for us" (Romans 5:8, Phillips), and why John could write, "We see real love, not in the fact that we loved God, but that he loved us and sent his Son to make personal atonement for our sins" (1 John 4:10, Phillips).

But that is not the whole story. Although Jesus died for our sins, He did not stay dead. God raised Him from the dead, thus robbing hell of any claim on Him and vindicating Jesus' work on man's behalf. The resurrection broke the power of sin, death, and hell over man and is the victorious climax to Jesus' life and ministry.

On the basis of Jesus' death and resurrection, God can freely forgive man, for the penalty has been paid by God Himself. But again, God does not force this pardon on anyone. We are not puppets. God offers forgiveness to us; it is up to us to accept or reject. The final point tells how we may appropriate the new life God offers.

4. *We may come to know God personally by receiving Christ as our Savior and Lord.* God's gift of forgiveness and eternal life is found in His Son. Thus, John states boldly, "God has given us eternal life, and this life is in His Son. He who has the Son has the life; he who does not have the Son of God does not have the life" (1 John 5:11b-12). How then may we have the Son? John answers, *by receiving him:* "But to all who received him, who believed in his name, he gave power to become children of God; who were born, not of blood nor of the will of the flesh nor of the will of man, but of God" (John 1:12-13, RSV).

Perhaps this is somewhat confusing. We have said that Jesus rose physically from the dead and then left the universe; He will return at the end of history. So how can one receive Him? I think the answer can be found in John's further explanation that those who received Him were born, not by physical means, but of God. That clearly refers to the spiritual birth discussed in John 3:1-13. In a conversation with a Jewish leader, Jesus stated that no one can enter the kingdom of God unless he is born again. The Jewish leader thought Jesus meant *physically* born again, which is impossible. So Jesus explained that He was talking about a *spiritual* rebirth. "Flesh gives birth to flesh and spirit gives birth to spirit" (John 3:6, Phillips). Jesus used the analogy of the wind: you cannot see the wind itself, but you can see its effects. "So is every one who is born of the Spirit" (John 3:8).

This discussion teaches that it is God's Spirit who causes the spiritual rebirth in the soul of a man. According to John, after Jesus' resurrection and departure from the world, the Spirit would take over Jesus' ministry here. Jesus said:

> And I will pray the Father and he will give you another Counselor, to be with you forever, even the Spirit of truth, whom the world cannot receive, because it neither sees him nor knows him; you know him, for he dwells with you, and will be in you. . . . I tell you the truth: It is to your advantage that I go away, for if I do not go away, the Counselor will not come to you; but if I go, I will send him to you. [John 14:16-17; 16:7, RSV]

It is clear that the Spirit would "stand in" for Jesus while Jesus was physically absent from this world. This implies, therefore, that when John talks about receiving Christ, he means, more technically, receiving the Spirit. When a man receives the Spirit of God, he is spiritually born again. The reason this can be spoken of as receiving Jesus is because the Spirit is acting on behalf of and in the role of Jesus.

That is confirmed by Paul's use of certain expressions. Notice how freely he interchanges "Spirit," "Spirit of Christ," "Christ":

> But you are not in the flesh, you are in the Spirit, if the Spirit of God really dwells in you. Any one who does not have the Spirit of Christ does not belong to him. But if Christ is in you, although your bodies are dead because of sin, your spirits are alive because of righteousness. [Romans 8:9-10, RSV]

Since the Spirit acts on behalf of Christ, He becomes so closely identified with Christ that He may be referred to simply as Christ.

Thus, it is by receiving God's Spirit that a man becomes a Christian. That fact may also be vividly seen by one's reading the book of Acts. Time and again we see that it is only when a person receives the Holy Spirit that he really becomes a Christian. James D. G. Dunn in his study of the Holy Spirit in the New Testament concludes,

The one thing which makes a man a Christian is the gift of the Spirit. Men can have been for a long time in Jesus' company, can have made profession of faith and been baptized in the name of the Lord Jesus, can be wholly 'clean' and acceptable to God, can even be 'disciples,' and *yet not be Christians*, because they lack and until they receive the Holy Spirit.[9]

Later Dunn remarks, "This has an important consequence, for it means that the thing which determines whether a man is a Christian is not his profession of faith in Christ but the presence of the Spirit."[10] That has shattering implications. It means clearly that one is not a Christian because he is a member of a church or is religious or follows the Golden Rule or even is a minister or priest. It is one of the greatest and most tragic errors of our day that most people think that a person is a Christian because he goes to church or believes certain doctrines or lives a good life. This notion, which is preached from thousands of church pulpits, is not true. *A person is a Christian only because he has received the Spirit of Christ and so has been born again.*

If a person has truly received Christ (i.e., the Spirit), he knows it. As Dr. Dunn remarks, the gift of the Spirit was a fact of experience for the early Christians, and it would be unthinkable for them that someone could have received the Spirit and yet not be aware of it.[11] For New Testament Christians, the reality of the Spirit in their lives was unmistakable. He was the source of power in their lives and gave them the firm assurance that they had been born again and were thus God's children. It is the same today for anyone who receives the Spirit and lives in His power.

When a person receives Christ, certain consequences of sin are eliminated. Let us review the three consequences we discussed before and see how each is removed when a person receives Jesus.

1. *He is forgiven of all his sin.* We saw that man stands morally guilty before God. But since God Himself in Jesus has borne the penalty for our sin, we need no longer be punished ourselves. God offers us complete and free

pardon. He promises, "I will have mercy on their transgressions and will no longer remember their sins" (Hebrews 8:12, RSV). In placing our trust in Jesus and receiving His Spirit, we receive God's gift of forgiveness. Thus, we are free from the bondage of evil that enslaved us, and free to live for God.

2. *His personal relationship with God is restored.* We saw that it was man's evil that separated him spiritually from God. But now that our sins are forgiven through Christ, the gulf separating us from God has been bridged. Jesus Himself is the bridge by means of which we come to God. In receiving Christ we come to have a personal relationship with God as our loving heavenly Father. Paul wrote,

> Nor are you meant to relapse into the old slavish attitude of fear—you have been adopted into the very family circle of God and you can say with a full heart, "Father, my Father". The Spirit himself endorses our inward conviction that we really are the children of God. [Romans 8:15-16, Phillips]

Perhaps the most wonderful gift that God gives to those who receive Christ is that they are adopted into the family of God.

3. *He is born again to new spiritual life.* Apart from God, man is spiritually dead. But when we receive the Spirit of God, we are spiritually born again to new life. Paul said, "You were spiritually dead. . . . But even though we were dead in our sins God, who is rich in mercy, because of the great love he had for us, gave us life together with Christ" (Ephesians 2:1, 4, Phillips). And Peter exclaims, "Blessed be the God and Father of our Lord Jesus Christ! By his great mercy we have been born anew to a living hope through the resurrection of Jesus Christ from the dead" (1 Peter 1:3, RSV). Where death and darkness once reigned, there is now life and light. If you have never received Christ, if you have never been born again by God's Spirit, then there is a whole plane of life and reality that you have not yet experienced. To be spiritually alive, to know God and walk with Him daily, is the greatest adventure that there is in life.

Thus, when a person receives the Spirit of Christ, his sins are forgiven, his personal relationship with God is restored, and he is born again to new spiritual life. "Thanks be to God for his inexpressible gift!" (2 Corinthians 9:15, RSV).

But if we may come to know God personally by receiving Jesus Christ, how do we go about receiving Him? According to the New Testament, there are only two conditions for receiving God's Spirit: repentance and faith.

Repentance means a genuine sorrow for one's evil acts and thoughts and a firm resolve to turn away from them to God. Repentance is a vital part of receiving Christ. When Jesus began His ministry, the first words that fell from His lips were: "The right time has come, and the Kingdom of God is near! Turn away from your sins and believe the Good News!" (Mark 1:15, TEV). It should be emphasized that repentance is not penance, such as making a pilgrimage or crawling on one's knees at some holy place. There is nothing we can do to *earn* forgiveness from God. Forgiveness is a gift, and all we can do is receive it with joy and gratitude. Repentance is an attitude of the heart, a disgust with one's sin and resolve to turn from it. It says to God, "Lord, I'm sick and tired of my sins and the way I am. I'm ready and willing to turn away from all of that."

Faith is wholehearted trust. Mere repentance does not save; it is through the extra step of placing one's trust in Jesus that one receives salvation. Paul said, "Believe in the Lord Jesus, and you will be saved" (Acts 16:31, RSV). It should be emphasized that faith is not simply giving intellectual assent to some doctrines. One can sincerely believe that Jesus is God's Son, that He died on the cross for one's sins, and that He rose from the dead, and still not be born again. The faith we are talking about is a commitment, a giving over, or a trusting of one's self to Jesus. It is that sort of personal trust that results in receiving the Spirit and being born again.

Thus, salvation is not something that we can earn. It is God's act in response to our turning from sin and our committing ourselves to Him to save us. Repentance and faith are not works that we do to earn salvation; they are just the lifting of the cup to receive God's lifegiving water. The

Bible calls this grace, God's unmerited favor. It is God's grace that saves us, as Paul explains: "For by grace you have been saved through faith; and this is not your own doing, it is the gift of God—not because of works, lest any man should boast" (Ephesians 2:8-9, RSV). This then is the proper understanding: God saves us *by* His grace *through* our faith *on the basis of* Jesus' sacrifice on the cross.

The whole operation of salvation is wonderfully summarized in this passage:

> For we ourselves have known what it is to be ignorant, disobedient and deceived, the slaves of various desires and pleasures, while our lives were spent in malice and jealousy— we were hateful and we hated each other. But when the kindness and love of God our saviour dawned upon us, he saved us in his mercy—not by virtue of any moral achievement of ours, but by the cleansing power of a new birth and the renewal of the Holy Spirit, which he poured upon us through Jesus Christ our Saviour. The result is that we are acquitted by his grace, and can look forward in hope to inheriting life eternal.
> [Titus 3:3-7, Phillips]

Here we clearly see (1) our sinful condition and need, (2) the love of God, which inspired our salvation, (3) our inability to earn that salvation, (4) the agency of the Holy Spirit in bringing about salvation by imparting new spiritual life, (5) the person of Jesus as our Savior, (6) the grace of God, which freely gives us what we did not deserve and could not earn, and (7) the result of salvation in our restored relationship with God and our having eternal life. (Praise the Lord!)

If you have never come to know God in a personal way and have not received Christ as your Savior and Lord, may I encourage you to do so now? Simply tell Him of how you regret your sin and turn from it; then in faith give yourself over to Christ. This can be done by prayer, which is just talking with God. Since many find it difficult to know what to pray, here is a suggested prayer—it is not so much the words that count as the attitude of the heart:

Lord, I admit that I am guilty before you because I have sinned. I am sorry for my sins and now turn from them to you. I give my life, all that I am, to you. Come into my life, forgive my sins, give me your Spirit, and make me the kind of person you want me to be. Thank you for answering this prayer, in the name of Jesus. Amen.

If you sincerely come to God with such an attitude in your heart as is expressed in this prayer, if you truly turn from your sin and believe, then you may be confident that God answers this prayer and sends His Spirit to you. You may not feel any different at first, but that is not the important factor. We are saved through faith in Christ, not through feelings. Feelings—such as the love, joy, and peace that the Spirit produces in a believer's life (Galatians 5:22-23)—will assuredly come as the Spirit makes His presence felt in your life. Sometimes others may notice the change in you before you do. Such feelings are confirmation that we have been born again; they are not the basis of that assurance. The basis of our assurance is the promise of God Himself: "WHOEVER WILL CALL UPON THE NAME OF THE LORD WILL BE SAVED" (Romans 10:13). If we sincerely turn to God in repentance and faith, believing that He will produce in us spiritual rebirth, then He will.

If you have just committed your life to Christ as your personal Savior and Lord, today marks your spiritual birthday, an event more significant than your physical birthday. Spiritually you are now like a newborn baby, and you need to be spiritually nourished and cared for. So begin to read your New Testament and talk to God daily. We speak to God in prayer, and He speaks to us in the Bible. Communicate often with your heavenly Father. If you sin, confess it to Him immediately, claiming the promise, "If we confess our sins, he is faithful and just, and will forgive our sins and cleanse us from all unrighteousness" (1 John 1:9, RSV). Tell someone about your decision to commit your life to Christ. That public witness to Christ is an outward evidence of the inward change in your heart. The New

Testament promises, "If you confess with your lips that Jesus is Lord and believe in your heart that God raised him from the dead, you will be saved. For man believes with his heart and so is justified, and he confesses with his lips and so is saved" (Romans 10:9-10, RSV). There is no such thing as a secret Christian.

Since you are part of God's family of sons and daughters, seek out a church where the Bible is preached and where you can make friends with other Christians. You should make this a matter of earnest prayer for God's guidance, since many churches today have departed from biblical Christianity and are sadly little more than social organizations. Visit different churches and look for one where salvation and spiritual rebirth by grace through faith is emphasized and where you sense the love, joy, and enthusiasm that the Holy Spirit brings.

Then you should ask to be baptized as an expression of your faith in Christ. Although most of us are accustomed to infant baptism, that is not the biblical pattern. The New Testament pattern is that a person first believes in Jesus and then is baptized as a public expression of that faith. Your baptism as a believer is in a sense the climax to your becoming a Christian and therefore ought not to be delayed indefinitely.

Finally, may I suggest that you write to Moody Correspondence School (2101 W. Howard St., Chicago, IL 60645) and ask about "The Good News," a home study Bible course to help you grow as a new Christian.

I wish you all God's richest blessings in your new life, a life that is possible because in the midst of the darkness of the night of sin, the Son has risen. "Now may the God of peace who brought again from the dead our Lord Jesus, the great shepherd of the sheep, by the blood of the eternal covenant, equip you with everything good that you may do his will, working in you that which is pleasing in his sight, through Jesus Christ; to whom be glory for ever and ever. Amen" (Hebrews 13:20-21, RSV).

NOTES

1. David C. K. Watson, *My God Is Real* (New York: Seabury, 1970), p. 60.
2. William Hordern, gen. ed., *New Directions in Theology Today*, 7 vols.; *History and Hermeneutics*, by Carl E. Braaten (London: Lutterworth Press, 1968), 2:80-81. Happily the situation has improved since Braaten wrote.
3. Gerald O'Collins, *The Easter Jesus* (London: Darton, Longman & Todd, 1973), p. 134.
4. See James D. G. Dunn, *Jesus and the Spirit* (London: SCM, 1975), pp. 11-92.
5. Ibid., p. 60.
6. Ibid., p.86.
7. Wolfhart Pannenberg, "Jesu Geschichte und unsere Geschichte," in *Glaube und Wirklichkeit* (München: Chr. Kaiser, 1975), p. 92.
8. Ibid., pp. 93-94. Elsewhere he writes, "Jesus' claim to authority, through which he put himself in God's place, was . . . blasphemous for Jewish ears. Because of this, Jesus was then also slandered by the Jews before the Roman Governor as a rebel. If Jesus really has been raised, this claim has been visibly and unambiguously confirmed by the God of Israel, who was allegedly blasphemed by Jesus." (Wolfhart Pannenberg, *Jesus: God and Man*, trans L. L. Wilkens and D. A. Priebe [London: SCM, 1968], p. 67.)
9. James D. G. Dunn, *Baptism in the Holy Spirit* (London: SCM, 1970), p. 93.
10. Ibid., p. 149.
11. Ibid., pp. 225-26.